Let's Preserve It

BERYL WOOD

Let's Preserve It

◨ SQUARE PEG

LONDON

Published by Square Peg 2011

6 8 10 9 7 5

First published in Great Britain by Souvenir Press 1970

Published in Great Britain in 2010 by
Square Peg
Random House, 20 Vauxhall Bridge Road,
London SW1V 2SA

www.randomhouse.co.uk

Addresses for companies within The Random House Group Limited can be found at:
www.randomhouse.co.uk/offices.htm

The Random House Group Limited Reg. No. 954009

A CIP catalogue record for this book
is available from the British Library

ISBN 9780224086738

The Random House Group Limited supports The Forest Stewardship
Council (FSC), the leading international forest certification organisation. All our titles that are
printed on Greenpeace approved FSC certified paper carry the FSC logo. Our paper procurement
policy can be found at www.randomhouse.co.uk/environment

Printed and bound in Germany by GGP Media GmbH, Pößneck

Foreword

When I first turned the pages of Beryl Wood's remarkable book, I was as struck by its astonishing range as I was by its history. Published in 1970, a time when the trend for cheap convenience food was well into its stride and state of the art technology was widely acknowledged as the way forward as the means to feed a growing population, Wood's collection of preserving recipes was a manifesto for safeguarding our grandmothers' artisan ways. Her book was a nudge that reminded not to walk past a hedgerow without collecting a few rosehips or blackberries during their season, nor miss a glut of cheaply abundant fruits or vegetables. She reminds us that making just a few pots of pickles, jam, jelly or fruit curd upholds a great and endangered tradition. She called the experience of opening a cupboard stocked with your own homemade preserves worthwhile, but she was not just talking about the economic benefit but of life's deep rooted, hand-me-down qualities – to be lost at our peril.

Her own upbringing and unconventional life explains her interest in traditional cooking. Beryl Wood grew up in Kent, the 'garden of England' where she remembered picking fruit for preserving at an early age. As an adult she was secretary to a progressive obstetrician in South Africa, Dr Grantly Dick-Read. When he and his family moved to Britain, she returned with them and added the care of their vegetable garden to her duties. Her off-beat career extended to a stint at pest control, working in a restaurant and also running an all-women car hire firm. Having decided to embark upon a book of preserves, she could not have taken a more exemplary route, combing libraries and bookshops for authentic recipes, but best of all prising grandmothers' recipes from families.

All is arranged in what is to my mind the easiest, most accessible recipe book format – an alphabetical listing by ingredient. When the season for each fruit, vegetable or nut arrives, it takes just a few seconds to look up at least one way to preserve it, and there is helpful cross-referencing to other sections in the book. There are nearly 600 recipes, from apple butter to wine jelly and finally Wood's 'XYZ end of season relish', a recipe that polishes off the unripened green tomatoes and last of the peppers no-one is ever sure what to do with. So much of the appeal lies in the brevity of the recipes. Anyone who can bring the contents of a pan to the boil and simmer it gently can follow this book. But above all this is a perfectly judged collection that contains the classics – raspberry jam, lemon curd and marrow chutney, for example – but also many intriguing curiosities. Red berries and orchard fruits are added through the summer season to a brandy-filled earthenware pot for Fruit Cockayne, ready to eat at Christmas; there is a sauce made from the peppery flavoured flowers of a nasturtium; a jam made from cucumbers and another from coconut and over forty ways to pot, pickle or preserve a wind-fallen apple. You can only imagine and fantasise about the history of these recipes; picture the eighteenth-century cook who dreamt up the idea of combining marrows with blackberries in a chutney, stirring the pot over a small flame, waiting for the contents to thicken enough to be ready for potting.

We cooks are more than ready for Beryl Wood's wonderful work again. The emergence of farmers' markets selling gluts of British vegetables, and the rediscovery of the fun in foraging and an interest in global flavours, has brought eclecticism back to cooking. Inspiration drawn from the creativity of chefs, both from eating out and watching their television spectacles, shows how a little herb-flavoured fruit jelly can transform the ordinary dish to the extraordinary. Concern for the economic climate, environment and health has further renewed and underpinned that interest. There is new relevance to a book of preserves that fits perfectly in our time. With Beryl Wood's unmatchable work, her encouraging voice and inspirational recipes, the words bland and British can never be linked again.

Rose Prince, London 2011

Acknowledgements

It would be impossible to acknowledge individually all the sources from which material has been obtained for this book, the hundreds of recipe books through which I have browsed, the kindly loan of so many of 'Granny's cookbooks', and the unlimited patience of countless librarians and booksellers in my searches for old volumes. To all of them, one big 'thank you'.

But my undying gratitude must go to my many friends who have been willing (or perhaps not so willing) guinea-pigs of my culinary experiments. As my husband grew or picked so many of the basic ingredients, his suffering has been entirely of his own making!

The Kestrel Pit,
Stibb, Nr Bude.
August 1970.

Contents

TO MY HUSBAND

*who always turns up the Ace of Diamonds at
Patience, which means a person who is fond of rural pursuits and
delights in planting – which is how this book came to be written.*

Introduction

Cooking today is totally different from that of our great-grandmothers, or even grandmothers, both in quantity and style, but we should not allow ourselves to lose many of their flavoursome and economical adjuncts to the family meals.

The trend has been for 'quick' foods accompanied by a glass jar or tin from the shelf of the supermarket round the corner, but it is satisfying to find a way of life that does not always revolve round the flick of the television switch or its equivalent. Home-baking has been making a big comeback, and the comfort of an open fire (even with smokeless fuel) with the delight of buttered fresh bread and muffins on a Sunday afternoon are once more being appreciated.

It seemed to me, however, that Granny's famous store-cupboard had been badly neglected. Perhaps it was the thought of 23kg (50lb) of marmalade or 11kg (25lb) of strawberry jam at one go, and few houses today have the space for such quantities, nor has the working wife time to handle them. But there is no need to make more than small manageable amounts with the day's chores (or as a change from painting a room at the weekend). The pleasure to be gained from opening a cupboard of your own homemade chutneys and jams, particularly of unusual varieties, is a very worthwhile experience.

My large library of cookery books yielded me only one or two recipes for preserves to every hundred or two others, so I set myself the task of collecting and annotating such recipes from all possible sources. Over the months the numbers swelled, the varieties became increasingly interesting and the cooking of them fascinating. And I realized there must be others who would enjoy the pleasure of making and trying out 'new' tastes or variations of a known recipe.

A day in the country can provide the basis for good jams, free for the picking from the hedges, a supply of nuts for Christmas and many other useful items of provender, all for the price of a health-giving spell in the open air. Sometimes a cheap and rather despised vegetable like the marrow can yield a most delicious curd for tarts or with toast for tea.

So I put them all together, in some cases three or four different ones for an individual product, and you can take your choice from the flavours you think most enjoyable to your palate and that of your family. As you gain experience, try out combinations of flavours for yourself – it is surprising how easy this is once you have mastered the basic principles.

In quoting the ingredients, I have listed the smallest practical quantities – it is so much easier to double than halve! In some cases, therefore, the recipes are very much trial quantities. Fruits and vegetables are in alphabetical order, cross-referencing as necessary, so if you like plums, prunes or tomatoes you will find them all together, whether a jam, jelly or pickle. Thus, no index.

This volume is devoted entirely to preserving that can be done with the basic tools found in every kitchen; you will find no mention of bottling, canning or deep-freezing because each of these methods requires special equipment or facilities. The only 'luxury' mentioned is a liquidizer, although even then a certain amount of sieving is necessary. But if you do not have one, a good

sieve and the strength of your wrists serves just as well, if perhaps
not so quickly and rather more tiring!

Having penned these few lines, there is nothing more to be said
but to get on with the job. Read carefully the points to remember
for the product you are making, then go to it – make great-grandma
proud that her work and ingenuity have not been forgotten in a
world of nuclear activity and landing on the Moon.

Equipment and Preparation

BASIC EQUIPMENT

HOUSEHOLD SCALES. These must be accurate.

PANS. If you are lucky enough to have a preserving pan or very large heavy saucepan, these are ideal, but whatever is used must have a solid base. For cheeses and curds, a double saucepan is useful, otherwise stand a bowl in a pan of boiling water. Copper and brass pans must NEVER be used for chutneys and pickles, and whatever the contents, if they are to stand overnight, do not leave in a metal container.

KNIVES. One large sharp knife, one small sharp knife and a finely serrated knife. The latter is useful for very fine slicing, unless you have a passion for using large knives.

GRATER, preferably with three grades of grating.

MINCER, with coarse and fine blades. Not strictly essential, but you probably have one anyway.

WOODEN SPOONS, one or more with long handles. Always use a wooden spoon for stirring. A perforated spoon is handy for skimming and removing stones as they come to the surface;

it avoids waste. And if you are lucky enough to have an angled spoon, this does help you to avoid burns from a 'bubbling' pan.

LIQUIDIZER AND FINE SIEVE or
1 COARSE SIEVE AND 1 FINE SIEVE

Odd pieces of muslin or old fine sheeting (boiled before use) for pips, pith and/or spices.

JUGS. A jug with a good wide-shaped lip for filling jars. A jam funnel does a cleaner job, but add this to your Christmas Tree list and hope someone will take the hint.

JARS. Plenty of them with wide mouths. It is very satisfying to see neat rows in uniform shape and size, but not always possible in the early stages. Over a period, however, you can collect your favourite brand of coffee jar (or similar); keep them well and cleanly stored. Small cream jars are useful for jellies – you can then use up a pot at a time and save clutter on everyday shelves. Additionally, of course, jelly is better stored in small quantities. If you want to make bulk amounts, then the old large stone jars are wonderful – they seem to have an additional keeping quality and chutneys mature marvellously in them. You can also collect interesting and unusual pots – I have some most attractive mussel jars which the local pub keeps for me.

COVERS. These can be purchased from most stationers in 450g (1lb) and 900g (2lb) sizes. Although a little pricey in the first place, I like paraffin wax – after use it is washed and returned to its kettle to be used again. Any small cheap kettle will suffice, but never use it for any other purpose once it has had the wax in it.

Grandma used circles tied down tightly and painted over with melted candle wax or, to seal vegetables, melted mutton fat.

LABELS. Always label and date the jars when they are cold. Ordinary sticky labels, self-adhesive labels or one of the labelling machines for which you can get gorgeous colours – they are all for the same purpose – to know the exact contents and the date on which it was made.

GENERAL PREPARATION AND COOKING HINTS

Never make a large quantity when trying a new recipe, even if the ingredients are cheap. Unless you are sure what the end taste will be, if you and your family don't like it, then time, money and energy have been wasted. Your local fête, however, will be delighted to take them off you to raise funds!

Fruit should be washed before cooking. If you neglect this, jam may go damp or mouldy and setting may be affected. Do this washing just before the fruit goes into the pan, allowing time to drain well. In the case of stoned fruit, just before you slit them (see below).

If fruit has to be stoned, it is quicker to slit the side and put whole into the pan. The stones will release themselves and rise to the surface during cooking, and can be removed with a perforated spoon. The fruit can be stoned first, but this is often messy, it takes time and a lot of valuable juice may be lost.

Always start cooking on a gentle heat to prevent sticking. Added ways to avoid this are to put a small knob of butter in the bottom of the pan before you start or, if one is available, a small marble. I also find that a heat diffuser under the pan in the early stages is a great help. Don't forget a gentle stir with a wooden spoon from time to time, unless specifically told not to.

Do not cover the pan at any stage during cooking unless the recipe says to do so.

Some fruits are low in pectin (see Pectin – Its Importance and Use) and therefore additives are needed for some jams and jellies. Where these ingredients are shown (i.e. lemon, commercial pectin) they must not be omitted if the jam is to set.

Whatever the preserve, when thickening is apparent, it is well on its way to being ready for bottling, and by this time you should have plenty of jars lined up. Over-estimate the number you will require – it is infuriating to get nearly to the bottom of the pan and then have to rush around collecting more containers. Make sure the jars are absolutely clean and put in a cool oven or warming drawer.

Have ready a clean surface near the stove, cover it with newspaper and when you are ready to pot, place the jars on this to fill them. The jars can then be wiped and removed, the newspaper rolled up and thrown away, and no sticky mess is left to be cleared up.

Most preserves are bottled when hot, unless otherwise noted.

Clean jars with a damp cloth whilst still warm.

Cover when hot or cold. If you are using the wax process the latter appears to be the most satisfactory, but do not use the wax too hot or it will crack the jars. If using jam covers, put the small wax circle on them when hot. Never cover preserves when just warm – mould may form.

When quite cold, label and store away in a cool dry place, preferably in the dark. Check the jars from time to time – if mould is forming the cupboard may be damp or too warm.

For your own sake, do try to be methodical. Collect together your ingredients and equipment before you start and clear as you go. A paper bag for throwing away husks and vegetable skins, etc., and a bowl of hot water into which you can drop spoons, squeezers, graters and the like as you finish with them; it saves a lot of hard work with washing-up.

Most of the above notes are really plain common sense and, basically, this is what preserving is all about, but it is sometimes a good thing to collect these ideas together in your own mind and then if the phone rings, the baby falls out of the cot or you cut yourself, these are just little irritations you will take in your stride. As every kitchen should always have a tin of first-aid dressings and a tube of Savlon handy, your cut or burn should take no more than half a stride.

PECTIN – ITS IMPORTANCE AND USE

Pectin is the most important factor of all in jam- and jelly-making. It is the substance which makes the set.

Contained in the walls of fruit and released during cooking, it acts with the natural acids and added sugar to form the set or jelly.

Most pectin is contained in slightly under-ripe fruits, a great deal is lost in over-ripe fruits and, generally speaking, fruit picked after a spell of wet weather is lower in pectin.

Test for Pectin
Simmer a small quantity of fruit till tender. Put a teaspoon of juice in small glass and when cold add 3 teaspoons methylated spirit.

Leave approximately 1 minute.

Fruit RICH in pectin will form a firm transparent jelly.
MEDIUM content of pectin will not be so firm a jelly.
LOW pectin content will leave a broken up jelly.

Hints for Low Pectin content
Use apple juice or lemon juice in quantities of 150ml (¼ pint)
apple juice or 2 tablespoons of lemon juice per 1.8kg (4lb) fruit.
Add at the beginning of cooking.

Commercial Pectin
Bottles of commercial pectin can be bought from chemists and
should be used as directed on the label, being added at the end
of the cooking process. When this is to be added to the fruit and
sugar, a very short cooking time only is needed but a fast, or full-
rolling, boil is an absolute must.

Guide to Pectin Content of Fruits

HIGH	MEDIUM	LOW
Apples	Apricots	Cherries
Blackcurrants	Blackberries	Elderberries
Cranberries	Greengages	Figs
Damsons	Loganberries	Medlars
Gooseberries	Peaches	Mulberries
Lemons	Plums (generally)	Pears
Acid Plums	Raspberries	Rhubarb
Quinces		Strawberries
Redcurrants		

2
Points to Remember

JAM-MAKING

Slightly under-ripe fruit is best. Over-ripe fruit loses its sugar content, may not set and is less likely to keep. Carefully sorted, however, fruit unsuitable for jam can be used for jellies (adding commercial pectin), chutneys and cheeses.

Do be accurate with weighing and measuring. The hit-and-miss variety of cooking does not belong to this department. A standard form of weights and measures has been used throughout so you will not have to worry about transposing cups to kilograms and litres, etc.

Use lump, granulated or preserving sugar in that order. The first dissolves a little quicker so if time is important use it, though it is a little more expensive. The last does not involve the same amount of 'skimming' as the other two. With rare exceptions, dark sugars are not good for jam – they change the colour of the fruit and tend to spoil their flavour.

Sugar warmed slightly before adding to the fruit will dissolve quicker and not reduce the heat so much. Long boiling detracts from flavour, spoils the colour, upsets the setting quality and does not help the keeping.

When adding the sugar keep stirring gently till it has all dissolved, then bring to the boil stirring occasionally to make sure it is not sticking.

Mention was made of a knob of butter to prevent sticking, but another use for butter is a small knob added just before removing from heat – it gives jam a shine and makes scum disappear.

When bringing jam to a full 'rolling' boil, this means it boils so hard that it spits. Keep at this temperature until it sets when tested.

For whole fruit jam, prepare fruit, put in a bowl with the sugar and stand overnight, then cook very slowly the next day.

Use synthetic sweeteners if you have someone in the family on a diet, using gelatine for setting. Make only small quantities at a time as it does not keep well.

Testing for Set

When thickening is apparent, lower heat and test for set. The easiest way is to drop a small spoonful on to a cold saucer and if, when cooled, it wrinkles to the touch, the jam is ready. If it does not set, bring to boil again for about three minutes and try again. DO NOT OVERBOIL. If you have a sugar thermometer the temperature should read 104°C (220°F).

Reasons for non-setting can be numerous, but if the fruit was over-ripe or undercooked before adding the sugar, try adding 2 tbs. lemon juice per 1.8kg (4lb) fruit and try again. But do not waste your cooking even if you have to cheat on your first try. Either add commercial pectin, or as a real cheat, some gelatine dissolved in boiling water. In the latter case the jam won't last long, but it can be used for puddings, etc., and only do this when ALL else has failed.

Whole fruit jams should be allowed to cool slightly before potting or the fruit will rise in the jar. Other jams should be bottled hot unless stated.

Pectin, acid and sugar must be balanced for a well-set jam – the released pectin affects the colour and flavour of the jam as well as sets it, so read the section on Pectin – Its Importance and Use.

Be sure the pan you use is of adequate size for the quantities being prepared. If it is too small, the jam will boil over the top (horrible mess) and you will have to turn it down too low to allow for proper cooking and evaporation, and again the jam will not set as it should.

If jam crystallizes, this may be caused by too much sugar, overboiling or storing in too dry a place. There is nothing you can do about it, but watch for these points next time.

This may seem a lot of reading, but once you have taken it in and made a few pots of jam, you will never have to turn to these pages again ...

JELLY-MAKING

The making of jellies is very simple but the overall time factor is longer than in jams or chutneys, because the straining of the juice must not be hurried.

If you have a jelly bag – good. They can be purchased from most household stores but they are not cheap. You can use a double thickness of muslin or sheeting very adequately and if necessary, strain twice for a clear juice.

Whatever you use, it must be absolutely clean and do not use detergents for the washing. If necessary, boil in clear fresh water, wring out well and dry, then scald again before use.

It does save wear on your jelly bag to strain through muslin first and then through the jelly bag.

An upturned kitchen stool makes a good stand for the bag, attaching the corners to the stool legs with a basin underneath. For safety, strain overnight, but even then keep out of the way of active children, rumbustious dogs and fruit-loving cats!

Never squeeze the jelly bag – it may make the juice cloudy. A good jelly should always be clear and bright.

Do not waste the pulp after you have strained the juice. Either put it through a liquidizer or sieve and use for a fruit butter or purée, having put it in a pan with a little more water first. Even when using the liquidizer, do put the purée through a sieve as well, since peels, cores, the lot were cooked up in the first place. Alternatively use straight away for a fool, flan or tart.

Testing for Set

Using a small spoon, take a small quantity of the syrup and if it drops from the spoon in large flakes, it is set. If it runs off the spoon, further boiling is necessary, but do not overboil, or the jelly will never set.

Although I have avoided using weight for liquids so far as possible, should you find a recipe that does, the easy method of doing this is to weigh the bowl, add liquid, weigh again and subtract the weight of the bowl. If you have digital scales you can reset to zero with the bowl on.

Once you have mastered the art of jelly-making, do be ambitious – try spicing them, use them lavishly with meat and even fish dishes – try spiced gooseberry with lamb and spiced grape with fish for example. Experiment by yourself if your family won't go with you in the first place. Sometimes a very plain dish with an interesting accompaniment is preferable to an exotic dish by itself.

CHUTNEYS AND PICKLES

On the whole, these are the easiest of all preserves, because the problem of setting as in jams and jellies does not apply but over-cooking must be avoided otherwise the chutney will dry out during storage and mould will form.

First, I must repeat, NEVER use a copper or brass pan for any chutneys or pickles.

Always use the best vinegar; it is false economy to do otherwise, but if you intend to do a lot of pickling and chutney making buy malt and white vinegar in bulk.

Choose good ripe, but not over-ripe, vegetables for a crisp chutney or pickle. If over-ripe they will lose themselves in the cooking, but do not discard them for this reason. You can still make a softer sweeter chutney which is excellent with cold meats.

Whole fruits for pickling should be pricked before heating to avoid shrivelling.

At the risk of being tedious, do not overboil. When a chutney thickens it is ready for bottling.

Both chutneys and pickles are always better for keeping. Try to give them at least a month before you open them, but if you can eventually manage to work a year ahead of demand, the proof of the chutney will be in the eating.

Cover chutneys in the same way as jams, but screw-top jars are preferable. If the lids are metal, then screw down over greaseproof paper. If you do happen to have some good stone jars, then cut corks to fit, and close down hard.

When pickling, the vegetables should be soaked in salt and water for at least 24 hours before cooking or, where no cooking is needed, before bottling.

Tie whole spices in a muslin bag before adding to vinegar. If you have to use ground spices, strain vinegar twice through muslin before adding to the pickles otherwise the liquid will be cloudy.

There is one particular note I would like to make concerning onions. Do not prepare them until you are ready for them to go into the pan. Cut onions should never be left lying around for health reasons, and this is worth remembering in all forms of cooking. If at any time you need only half an onion, wrap the other half in foil and put in the fridge; don't just throw it back into the vegetable rack. The explanation for this is very technical and a digression into a chemistry lesson is not appropriate here.

In some recipes you may find ingredients you do not normally keep on the shelf. However, if you gradually build up a good spice and herb rack, you will be surprised at the number of other uses you will find for them, and the variety of flavours you can obtain from comparatively cheap and otherwise dull dishes. (Do you add mixed spice to a stew and herbs to a Yorkshire pudding? – try them and see the difference.)

FRUIT BUTTERS AND CHEESES

These are a wonderful way of making use of over-ripe fruit and the pulp left after straining juices for jelly.

The main difference between the two is that a butter is of a creamy type consistency and does not last as long as a cheese, which uses more sugar and is a much stiffer consistency.

There is very little to say about them, they are simple to make, keep well according to the amount of sugar used, and taste delicious. They are very good for people who do not like jam with pips in. Butters can be used ideally with hot puddings.

DRYING

A number of vegetables can be dried very satisfactorily, as can some fruits, but it is a process which takes time and you must not be irritated by odd trays of things standing around. It is also disastrous if you have left them in a cooling off oven and forgot to remove them again when you turn on the heat! Nevertheless, in the summer good use can be made of any sun we may have and any airtight container can be used for storage. But it is absolutely essential that the fruit or vegetable is fully dried out before being stored otherwise they will go mouldy.

Into this category come herbs, of course, probably the most commonly done, take little space and have a constant use in the kitchen. Fresh picked, tied in small bundles and hung in free air, they do themselves. For the most part it is country people who will have most opportunity to do this, but there is no reason why you shouldn't grow various herbs in a window box, and then dry them against the time when the fresh variety will not be available.

The preceding pages cover the general principles that apply to the recipes in this book. There is much more that could be said. For the history of this form of cooking or non-cooking, as the case may be, is interesting and varied. However it would take a small encyclopedia to do this and there are so many other things that could also be done if space would allow, fruit syrups for example.

But the recipes that have resulted from history are more important than the history itself in the first place, so collect the family, set them gathering, and a plentiful and fruitful store cupboard to you.

3.
The A–Z Recipes for Preserving Fruits and Vegetables

A

APPLE BUTTER (American Style)

Apples, cloves, allspice, cinnamon, sweet cider.

Peel, core and quarter apples; put in pan, just cover with good sweet cider; add spices to personal taste; bring slowly to boil, mashing with wooden spoon till juice is absorbed, and you have a dark brown jam; when soft and buttery, pot and seal. (Keeping quality varies according to apples used.)

APPLE CHEESE

Apples, sugar, water.

Quarter apples, without peeling or coring; put in pan with small quantity of water; simmer till soft; put through liquidizer and sieve or 2 sieves; return to pan allowing 1kg sugar for each kilogram pulp (1lb per lb pulp), stirring till dissolved; boil rapidly till fairly stiff.

APPLE CHUTNEY

There are many variations of apple chutney, but the cooking principle is the same and very simple. The apples should be peeled, cored and coarse chopped together with any other fruit or vegetables used, the whole spices tied in a muslin bag; put all ingredients in pan, simmer gently for about 1 h or until mixture thickens, remove muslin bag, then pot and seal.

(1) *1.8kg (4lb) sour apples, 450g (1lb) sultanas, 225g (½lb) onions, 910g (2lb) soft brown sugar, 850ml (1½ pints) malt vinegar, rind and juice of 1 lemon, tbs. mustard seed, dsp. ground ginger.*

(2) *450g (1lb) sour apples, 450g (1lb) onions, 340g (¾lb) brown sugar, 570ml (1 pint) vinegar, 14g (½oz) each ginger, turmeric and curry powder, salt to taste.*

(3) *910g (2lb) cooking apples, 910g (2lb) brown sugar, 225g (½lb) raisins, 850ml (1½ pints) malt vinegar, 225g (½lb) green ginger [or 84g (3oz) bruised root ginger], 1tbs. mustard seed, 28g (1oz) garlic, a few blanched almonds and small chillies, salt to taste.*

(4) *1.6kg (3½lb) apples, 450g (1lb) onions, 450g (1lb) each raisins, currants and sultanas, 340g (¾lb) brown sugar, 56g (2oz) ground ginger, 28g (1oz) salt and mustard seed, 7g (¼oz) cayenne and mixed spice, 2l (3½ pints) malt vinegar.*

(5) *910g (2lb) apples, 450g (1lb) onions, 340g (¾lb) brown sugar, 570ml (1 pint) malt vinegar, 113g (¼lb) dried fruit (sultanas or raisins), 1tsp. each pickling spice, ground ginger and salt.*

APPLE CURD

*680g (1½lb) sour apples, 2 eggs, 113g (¼lb) butter, 340g (¾lb)
caster sugar, juice 1 lemon, 150ml (¼ pint) water,
¼tsp. ground ginger.*

Peel, core and rough chop apples; simmer with little water and lemon juice till pulpy; liquidize or sieve; return to pan with remaining ingredients; heat mixture, stirring constantly, till it thickens but do not allow to boil. Pot and cover at once.

APPLE RINGS DRIED

*Ripe firm cooking apples, Brine [28g (1oz) salt,
4.5l (1 gallon) water].*

Peel apples, core through centre, cut in rings; throw into brine; stand 15 min; drain and dry; put on sponge rack without rings touching, or thread on sticks balanced over cake tin, without touching each other or the side of the tin; leave in cool oven for about 12 h.

Apple rings can also be threaded on a string and strung high in a warm atmosphere, provided the air is dry; if the weather is good, string them out in the sun.

APPLE GINGER

*910g (2lb) hard green apples, 910g (2lb) preserving sugar,
570ml (1 pint) water, 28g (1oz) ginger essence
or ground ginger.*

Peel, core and slice apples; put in bowl, cover with sugar and water; stand overnight; drain liquid into pan; boil for 20 min to a thin syrup, stirring to prevent sticking; add apple and ginger; boil quickly till apple becomes transparent; stir frequently but take care to leave apple slices intact; when clear, remove apple gently to warm jars, cover with syrup; cover down tightly while hot.

APPLE JAM

Cooking apples, preserving sugar, water, whole cloves.

Peel, core and thinly slice apples; weigh and put in pan with small quantity of water and 4 cloves per kilogram fruit (2 cloves per lb) tied in muslin bag; cook gently till apples are tender; remove from heat, cool, remove bag of cloves; put fruit through liquidizer or sieve; return to pan with 750g sugar per original kilogram apples, stirring till dissolved; boil approx. 1 h until mixture is firm when tested on cold plate; stir frequently throughout and skim as necessary.

APPLE JELLY

Apples, water, sugar.

This is a wonderful 'user-up' as it can be made from peel, cores, windfalls, etc., but do not use any bruised pieces. Keep the pulp after straining, return to pan with a little water to soften and continue as for Apple Butter or cheese. In this way, everything is used except a little roughage in your sieve. Quarter apples, removing any bruised parts; put in pan with little water; simmer till tender; strain through jelly bag; return liquid to pan, allow 800g sugar for each litre juice (1lb per pint), stirring till dissolved; boil fast to set. This is a good basic jelly which can be flavoured as desired, with lemon, ginger or other spices.

APPLE KETCHUP SPICED

910g (2lb) apples (when peeled and cored), 1large onion,
113g (¼lb) sugar, 210ml (⅜ pint) malt vinegar, 1tsp.
salt, ½tsp. curry powder, cayenne pepper and turmeric,
1tsp. pickling spice and 1 clove garlic (both tied in muslin bag).

Put all ingredients, except sugar, into pan and cook till apples are thick pulp; remove muslin bag; liquidize or sieve; return to pan, add sugar and boil rapidly for 10 min. Bottle and seal. (N.B. If you want this ketchup for keeping it must be sterilized, but it will keep a limited time without.)

APPLE MARMALADE

Apples, Butter, Sugar, Lemons.

Peel, core, chop and weigh apples; allow 1kg sugar, ½kg butter and the juice and rind of 2 lemons for each kilogram (1lb sugar, ½lb butter, rind 1 lemon per lb apples). Put apple, butter and ¼ of the sugar into double boiler (or basin in boiling water); simmer till fruit is tender; sieve, return to pan with rind and juice of lemon and remaining sugar, stirring till dissolved; boil gently till mixture thickens, stirring frequently and skimming if necessary; pot and cover closely at once.

APPLE PASTE

1.4kg (3lb) apples, water to cover, soft brown sugar.

Remove bruises and blemishes from apples and rough chop without peeling or coring; put in large pan with water to cover; simmer till apples are soft; liquidize and/or sieve; return to pan allowing 1kg sugar per 1kg purée (1lb sugar per lb purée), stirring constantly till quite stiff. Pot and cover. (This preserve does not keep for long, but if you have deep-freezing space, put in a carton and keep for future use.)

APPLE PASTE SPICED

910g (2lb) apples, 570ml (1 pint) dry cider,
450g (1lb) soft brown sugar.

Rough chop apples, put in fireproof dish with all ingredients in oven, very low, for 2–3 h; liquidize and/or sieve; put in preserving pan, stir over moderate heat till bubbling and reduced to about 850ml (1½ pints); pot and cover immediately.

APPLE PASTE SPICED AND SWEET

Follow recipe above using sweet instead of dry cider.

APPLE PICKLE (1)

450g (1lb) apples, 225g (½lb) onions, 570ml (1 pint) white
vinegar,1tbs. salt, 14g (½oz) peppercorns, a few chillies.

Peel, core and cut apples and onions; pack in jar with a few chillies; boil vinegar with salt and peppercorns; pour over fruit; cover when cold.

APPLE PICKLE (2)

910g (2lb) cooking apples, 4 shallots, 570ml (1 pint) vinegar,
113g (¼lb) sugar, 1tsp. turmeric, ½tsp. each ground ginger and
mustard, 2 cloves, 6 peppercorns (muslin bag), salt.

Peel, core and cube apples; spread on dish, cover with salt, stand overnight; drain, put in pan with chopped onion and all other ingredients; bring to boil, simmer till apple is tender but not mashed; remove bag of cloves and peppercorns before potting.

APPLE PICKLE (3)

450g (1lb) sharp apples, 225g (½lb) sugar, 210 ml (⅜ pint) cider vinegar, 1tsp. each allspice and cinnamon, small piece of root ginger and 6 cloves (in muslin bag).

Peel, core and cube apples; put vinegar, sugar and spices in pan, cover and simmer 10 min; add apples; simmer till tender; gently remove fruit to warmed jar; boil vinegar till syrupy, then remove muslin bag and pour syrup over the apples completely covering them; close down immediately; keep at least 8 weeks before using.

APPLES SPICED

Crab apples, vinegar, sugar (or use small cooking apples).

Remove stalks from unbruised apples, prick all over with fine needle and pack into jar; make syrup in the ratio of 1.6kg sugar to 1l vinegar (2lb to 1 pint); pour hot over fruit and cover closely.

APPLE STRUPER

910g (2lb) cooking or crab apples, 570ml (1 pint) water, sugar, honey, grated nutmeg, mixed spice or cinnamon.

Wash and halve apples; put in pan with water; simmer till pulped; strain through jelly bag; return to pan with 800g sugar (or 600g sugar and 200g honey), ½tsp. nutmeg and mixed spice (or cinnamon), to each litre juice (1lb per pint); boil to set. (If you do not necessarily want a clear jelly, you can liquidize the fruit and strain through sieve instead of using a jelly bag.)

APPLE AND APRICOT CHUTNEY

910g (2lb) cooking apples, 113g (4oz) dried apricots, 225g (½lb) onions, 225g (½lb) sultanas, 225g (½lb) soft brown sugar, 285ml (½ pint) vinegar, dsp. salt, pinch cayenne.

Soak apricots overnight; drain and chop; peel, core and slice apples; put all ingredients in pan, bring to boil, stirring; simmer about 30 min or till thickened.

Apple and Apricot Jam *see under Apricot.*

APPLE AND BANANA CHUTNEY

910g (2lb) apples, 1 doz. bananas, 340g (¾lb) onions, 225g (½lb) raisins, 56g (2oz) salt, 1tsp. cinnamon and ground ginger, 28g (1oz) curry powder, 570ml (1 pint) vinegar.

Peel, core and finely chop apples; finely chop onions; peel and slice bananas roundways; put all ingredients in pan and simmer very gently for about 1½ h stirring frequently until thick and fruit is tender.

Apple and Banana Jam *see under Banana.*
Apple and Blackberry Chutney; Apple and Blackberry Jam *see under Blackberry.*
Apple and Blackcurrant Jelly; Apple and Blackcurrant Jam *see under Blackcurrant.*
Apple, Carrot and Peach Marmalade *see under Carrot.*
Apple and Cherry Jam *see under Cherry.*

APPLE AND CLOVE JAM

Follow recipe for Apple Ginger (p5), substituting 6½ whole cloves or 1tsp. ground cloves per kilogram fruit (½tsp. per lb), omitting the ginger.

Apple and Cranberry Jelly; Apple and Cranberry Sauce *see under Cranberry.*
Apple and Damson Jam; Apple and Damson Jelly *see under Damson.*
Apple and Date Chutney *see under Date.*

APPLE DATE PRESERVE

*450g (1lb) cooking apples (when peeled and cored),
170g (6oz) stoned dates, 450g (1lb) sugar, juice 1 lemon.*

Put apples in bowl, cover with sugar and lemon juice; stand overnight; put into pan on low heat, stirring till sugar is dissolved, add chopped dates; cook to thick set.

Apple and Elderberry Jam; Apple and Elderberry Jelly *see under Elderberry.*
Apple and Fig Jam *see under Fig.*

APPLE FIG PRESERVE

Follow recipe for Apple Date Preserve, substituting 113g (4oz) dried figs for the 170g (6oz) stoned dates, soaking them overnight.

APPLE AND GERANIUM JELLY

Follow basic recipe for Apple Jelly, adding 4 or 6 fragrant geranium leaves with each kilogram of apples.

APPLE GINGER JAM (1)

*1.1kg (2½lb) cooking apples (when peeled and cored),
285ml (½ pint) water, 910g (2lb) sugar, 1–2tsp. ground
ginger (or piece root ginger).*

Peel and core apples, putting peelings and core in muslin bag,
with root ginger (if used instead of ground ginger); put apples,
water and muslin bag in pan; simmer till soft; remove muslin bag;
mash apples to smooth pulp; add sugar and boil steadily till set.

APPLE GINGER JAM (2)

*910g (2lb) cooking apples, 285ml (½ pint) water,
113g (4oz) preserved ginger, 1 lemon, 3 tbs. ginger syrup,
680g (1½lb) sugar.*

Peel and core apples, putting peelings and cores in muslin bag;
put apples, water and bag in pan; simmer till soft; remove muslin
bag, mash apples, add sugar, grated rind and juice of lemon, ginger syrup and chopped ginger; bring to boil stirring constantly;
boil 10 min or to set; pot and cover immediately.

APPLE GINGER JAM (3)

*450g (1lb) cooking apples, 450g (1lb) sugar,
1tsp. ground ginger.*

Peel and core apples, putting peelings and cores in muslin bag; put
all together in a bowl, cover with sugar, stand overnight; transfer
to pan, simmer gently, stirring till sugar is dissolved; add ginger,
boil steadily till apple is transparent and syrup sets; remove muslin bag; pot and cover immediately.

Apple and Greengage Jam *see under Greengage.*
Apple and Green Tomato Chutney *see under Tomato (green).*
Apple and Green Pepper Chutney *see under Pepper (green).*
Apple and Lemon Curd *see under Lemon.*

APPLE LEMON JAM

*450g (1lb) cooking apples (peeled and cored), 150ml (¼ pint)
water, 450g (1lb) sugar, grated rind and juice of 1 lemon.*

Follow recipe for Apple Ginger Jam.

APPLE LEMON JELLY

*450g (1lb) cooking apples, 2 lemons,
285ml (½ pint) water, sugar.*

Chop apples without peeling or coring, pare rind off lemons; put
both into pan with water and simmer till soft; strain through jelly
bag; add squeezed juice of lemons; put in pan with 800g sugar
per litre juice (1lb per pint), boil rapidly to set.

Apple and Lemon Marmalade *see under Lemon.*

APPLE AND MINT CHUTNEY

Follow recipe for Apple Chutney (4) adding 1dsp. fresh chopped
mint for each 450g (1lb) of apples.

Apple and Mulberry Jam; Apple and Mulberry Jelly *see under
Mulberry.*

APPLE AND ONION PICKLE

*340g (¾lb) cooking apples (when peeled and cored),
340g (¾lb) onions, 56g (2oz) sultanas, 425ml (¾ pint)
vinegar, 9 peppercorns, 9 cloves, 42g (1½oz) dried chillies,
2–3tsp. salt.*

Finely chop apples and onions, add sultanas, pack into warmed jar; put spices and chillies into muslin bag; steep in vinegar ½ h; bring to boil, simmer 10 min; pour hot into jar or jars to cover contents; tie down.

APPLE AND ORANGE CHUTNEY

*910g (2lb) cooking apples (peeled and cored), 1 orange,
225g (½lb) raisins, 450g (1lb) sugar,
850ml (1½ pints) vinegar.*

Finely chop apples and raisins; wipe orange, squeeze juice, remove pith, and chop peel finely; put fruit and peel in pan with 570ml (1 pint) vinegar; simmer with lid on till apples are soft; add orange juice, remaining vinegar and sugar, stirring till dissolved; boil gently till thickened.

Apple and Orange Curd *see under Orange*.

APPLE ORANGE JAM

Follow recipe for Apple Lemon Jam using the grated rind and juice of 2 oranges instead of the lemon.

APPLE AND ORANGE JELLY

Follow recipe for Apple Lemon Jelly using 2 oranges instead of the lemons.

Apple and Pear Jam *see under Pear.*

APPLE AND PINEAPPLE JAM

*450g (1lb) cooking apples (when peeled and cored),
450g (1lb) fresh pineapple (when peeled), 910g (2lb) sugar,
70ml (⅛ pint) water.*

Rough chop fruit, put in pan with water; simmer till soft; add sugar, stirring till dissolved; boil rapidly to set.

APPLE AND PLUM CHEESE

1.4kg (3lb) apples, 450g (1lb) plums, sugar, water.

Stalk and wash apples, and rough chop; put in pan with little water, simmer till nearly tender; slit plums, add to apple, continue cooking till soft; remove plum stones, liquidize and sieve, or sieve twice; return to pan with 600g sugar per litre pulp (¾lb per pint); bring to boil, stirring till sugar dissolved; boil steadily to set.

Apple and Plum Chutney *see under Plum.*

APPLE AND PLUM JELLY

910g (2lb) apples, 1.4kg (3lb) plums, sugar, water.

Wash apples, slice without peeling or coring; halve plums; put fruit in pan with 710ml (1¼ pints) water; simmer till tender; strain through jelly bag; return juice to pan with 800g sugar per litre liquid (1lb per pint); bring to fast boil; boil to set.

Apple, Pear and Plum Marmalade *see under Plum.*

APPLE AND PUMPKIN JAM

*910g (2lb) apples (when peeled and cored), 910g (2lb)
pumpkin (when peeled), 285ml (½ pint) water, sugar, cloves
or ginger as preferred.*

Peel, pith, seed and cut pumpkin in cubes; peel, core and rough slice apples; put fruit in pan with water and spice (tied in muslin); simmer till tender; remove muslin bag; liquidize or sieve fruit; return to pan with 800g sugar per litre purée (1lb per pint), stirring till sugar dissolved; boil fast for 15 min or to set.

Apple and Quince Jam; Apple and Quince Jelly *see under Quince.*
Apple, Quince and Cranberry Jelly *see Paradise Jelly.*
Apple and Redcurrant Jelly *see under Redcurrant.*

APPLE AND RHUBARB JAM

*450g (1lb) apples, 450g (1lb) rhubarb, 910g (2lb) sugar,
70ml (⅛ pint) water.*

Peel, core and chop apples; trim and chop rhubarb; put fruit in pan with water, simmer very gently till tender; add sugar, stirring till dissolved; boil rapidly to set.

Apple and Sloe Jelly *see under Sloe.*
Apple and Green Tomato Chutney *see under Tomato (green).*
Apple and Red Tomato Chutney; Apple and Red Tomato Jam
see under Tomato.

APPLE AND WALNUT CHUTNEY

910g (2lb) cooking apples, 56g (2oz) chopped walnuts,
225g (½lb) sultanas, 450g (1lb) soft brown sugar, 1 large
orange, 1 small lemon, 425ml (¾ pint) vinegar, 2 cloves.

Peel, core and finely chop apples; grate rinds of orange and lemon, squeeze juices and strain; put all ingredients into pan, bring to boil, simmer gently 1 h or till thick, stirring from time to time.

Apple *see also Autumn Chutney, Indian Relish.*

APRICOT BUTTER

910g (2lb) apricots, sugar, lemon, cinnamon, cloves, allspice.

Wash, peel and stone fruit; put in pan with very little water; simmer slowly till soft; liquidize or sieve; return to pan allowing grated rind and juice of 2 lemons, 2tsp. cinnamon and cloves, 1tsp. allspice and 400g sugar per litre purée (½lb per pint); cook slowly, stirring frequently, till thick.

APRICOT CHUTNEY

225g (½lb) dried apricots, 450g (1lb) apples (when peeled and
cored), 113g (4oz) stoned raisins, 113g (4oz) sultanas, 450g
(1lb) dark brown sugar, 570ml (1 pint) vinegar, 3tsp. pickling
spice, 1tsp. salt, juice and rind 1 lemon,
2 cloves garlic (if liked).

Chop apricots and soak overnight; drain, put in pan with chopped apples and raisins and all other ingredients except sugar (spices tied in muslin bag); simmer 30 min, add sugar, stirring till dissolved, then boil gently about 20 min or till thick.

APRICOT CONSERVE

450g (1lb) apricots, 450g (1lb) sugar, juice 1 lemon.

Quarter and stone apricots, put in pan with sugar and juice of lemon; heat very gently, stirring constantly till sugar is dissolved; boil slowly till set.

APRICOT CONSERVE (Dried Fruit)

450g (1lb) dried apricots, 2 oranges, 56g (2oz) seedless raisins, juice of 2 lemons, 1.7l (3 pints) water, 1.4kg (3lb) sugar.

Put apricots in bowl with water; slice oranges (put pips in muslin), add to apricots; stand for 48 h; put in pan, simmer slowly till soft; add sugar stirring till dissolved; add raisins and remove muslin bag; boil rapidly to set. [56g (2oz) walnuts can be added before potting if liked.]

APRICOT CURD

225g (½lb) apricots, 1 lemon, 225g (½lb) caster sugar, 56g (2oz) butter, 2 eggs, water.

Wash fruit and slit, put in pan with very little water; cook slowly till tender; remove stones, put fruit through liquidizer or coarse sieve; put into double saucepan (or bowl over boiling water) with sugar, butter, juice and rind of lemon, stirring till sugar dissolved;

add beaten eggs, stirring constantly till mixture thickens; pot and cover immediately.

APRICOT CURD (Dried Fruit)

Follow recipe as above, using 170g (6oz) dried apricots and soak for at least 24 h before cooking.

APRICOT JAM (Fresh Fruit)

I have eight different recipes for this jam, but for simplicity and a good result, I prefer the following:

910g (2lb) slightly under-ripe apricots, 1 lemon, 1.8kg (4lb) sugar, 425ml (¾ pint) water.

Halve and stone apricots and chop roughly; put in pan with water and juice of the lemon; simmer till tender; slowly add sugar, stirring all the time; bring to boil, and boil steadily till set. If desired a few blanched almonds can be added before potting.

APRICOT JAM (Dried Fruit)

450g (1lb) apricots, 1.8kg (4lb) sugar, 28g (1oz) almonds, 1.7l (3 pints) water.

Wash fruit, rough chop and soak in water 48 h; put in pan together with water in which soaked, boil for 15 min; add sugar, stirring till dissolved; bring to boil, stirring constantly; skim as necessary, cook till thick; remove from heat, add almonds; pot and cover. [A pleasant variation is to add the juice of 4 lemons for each kilogram of fruit (2 lemons per lb).]

APRICOT MARMALADE

*450g (1lb) stoned apricots, 340g (¾lb) sugar,
150ml (¼ pint) water.*

Put apricots in pan with water and simmer till soft; liquidize or sieve; return to pan with sugar, bring to boil and cook till set.

APRICOTS PICKLED

450g (1lb) apricots, 225g (½lb) sugar, 150ml (¼ pint) white or cider vinegar, 7g (¼oz) each allspice, cloves, mace, cinnamon and nutmeg [or 35 g (1¼oz) mixed spice].

Peel apricots, put in pan with sugar, spices and vinegar; bring to boil, simmer 5 min; remove fruit carefully and put in jar; simmer syrup till it thickens, pour hot over fruit to cover and close down tightly.

APRICOTS PICKLED (Dried Fruit)

*450g (1lb) dried apricots, 850ml (1½ pints) white vinegar,
570 g (1¼lb) sugar, 14g (½oz) each allspice and cloves, and
12mm (½in) cinnamon stick (all in muslin bag).*

Wash apricots and soak overnight; put vinegar and spice bag in pan, bring slowly to boil; drain apricots, add to vinegar and spices and simmer 5 min or till tender; remove fruit to jar; add sugar to vinegar, bring to boil stirring, and boil till syrupy; remove spice bag, pour syrup hot over the fruit to cover completely, then seal down firmly, preferably with a screw-top lid.

APRICOT AND ALMOND CONSERVE

Follow recipe for Apricot Conserve, adding 56g (2oz) blanched and chopped almonds when set is reached.

Apricot and Apple Chutney *see under Apple*.

APRICOT AND APPLE JAM

740 g (26oz) tin of apricots, 340g (¾lb) apples (when peeled and cored), 1.4kg (3lb) sugar, 1 lemon, 1 bottle commercial pectin.

Drain apricots, slice apples; put in pan with 150ml (¼ pint) apricot syrup, add sugar and juice of lemon, heating very slowly and stirring all the time till sugar is dissolved; bring quickly to boil, boil hard for 2 min; remove from heat; add pectin, stir for 5 min to prevent fruit rising, skimming as necessary.

APRICOT AND CHERRY JAM

910g (2lb) stoned apricots, 450g (1lb) stoned cherries, 1.4kg (3lb sugar), 2 lemons, 150ml (¼ pint) water (or little less if fruit is fairly ripe).

Put fruit in pan with water; simmer till tender; add sugar and lemon juice; stir till sugar is dissolved; boil rapidly to set.

APRICOT AND LEMON MARMALADE

*450g (1lb) dried apricots, 450g (1lb) lemons, 1.4kg (3lb)
sugar, 1.7l (3 pints) water.*

Finely slice lemons (putting pips in muslin bag); put in bowl with apricots and water; stand overnight; remove to pan, simmer till soft; add sugar, stirring till dissolved; boil rapidly to set.

Apricot and Marrow Jam *see under Marrow.*

APRICOT AND ORANGE MARMALADE

*225g (½lb) dried apricots, 2 oranges, 1.1kg (2½lb)
sugar, 1 lemon, 850ml (1½ pints) water.*

Follow procedure as for Apricot and Lemon Marmalade.

APRICOT AND PINEAPPLE JAM

*450g (1lb) ripe apricots, 450g (1lb) sugar, small
can pineapple chunks.*

Halve and stone apricots, cover with sugar; stand 2–3 h; crack stones and remove kernels; drain pineapple chunks; put apricots, sugar and 150ml (¼ pint) pineapple juice into pan, bring slowly to boil, stirring constantly and skimming as necessary; add pineapple and kernels; cook very slowly till fruit is transparent and syrup thick.

Apricot and Pineapple Preserve *see under Pineapple.*

APRICOT AND WALNUT JAM

Use recipe for Apricot Jam (fresh or dried fruit) adding 56g (2oz) finely chopped walnuts.

Apricots *see also Dried Fruit Pickle, Mixed Pickled Fruits.*

AUBERGINE CHUTNEY

910g (2lb) aubergine (when peeled), 340g (¾lb) onions, 450g (1lb) cooking apples (when peeled and cored), 570 g (1¼lb) dark brown sugar, 285ml (½ pint) vinegar, 2tsp. ginger, 2tsp. pickling spice (in muslin bag), 1tsp. salt.

Peel and cut aubergine in thin slices; chop onions very finely; peel, core and rough chop apples; put all ingredients (except sugar) into pan and simmer till tender; remove spice bag, stir in sugar and boil till thick.

AUBERGINE PICKLED

Aubergine, carrots, garlic, celery strands, spiced vinegar.

Cut aubergine lengthwise in half, scald in boiling water; drain well; finely chop carrot and garlic together and scald; stuff aubergine halves with carrot mixture; put halves together and tie with strands from outside the celery sticks; stand neatly in jar; pour over cold spiced vinegar; cover very closely.

AUBERGINE AND CAPSICUM (PEPPER) CHUTNEY

*2 aubergines, 2 peppers (green, red or 1 of each), 113g (4oz)
shallots, clove, peeled garlic, 425ml (¾ pint) vinegar, 1 apple,
56g (2oz) brown sugar, 1tsp. curry powder, 25mm (1in)
cinnamon stick, 25mm (1in) root ginger, 1 bay leaf, olive oil,
salt and turmeric.*

Cut aubergine and peppers in strips, removing seeds; rub with
salt and turmeric; mix curry powder with little vinegar, add cinnamon, ginger and bay leaf; leave 15 min; fry cut vegetables,
including sliced shallots and garlic for 10 min, stirring occasionally; add sugar, and peeled chopped apple; cook further 10 min;
add curry mixture and vinegar; simmer till thick; add salt to taste;
remove cinnamon, ginger and bay leaf before potting.

AUTUMN CHUTNEY

*450g (1lb) each stoned plums, peeled and cored apples,
tomatoes, onions, sultanas and Demerara sugar, 570ml (1 pint)
vinegar, 1 clove garlic (peeled and chopped), ¼tsp. each mace
and mixed spice, 28g (1oz) ground ginger.*

Coarsely chop vegetables and fruit, put in pan with all other
ingredients (except sugar) and simmer till tender; add sugar,
stirring till dissolved; cook till thick.

B

BANANA JAM

*450g (1lb) bananas (when peeled), 570ml (1 pint) apple juice,
225g (½lb) sugar, juice of 1 lemon.*

Peel and slice bananas; put apple juice, sugar and juice of lemon
in pan; bring to boil, stirring till sugar is dissolved; add bananas;
stir till boiling again and then cook slowly till mixture thickens;
pot and cover hot.

BANANA AND APPLE JAM

*450g (1lb) bananas, 225g (½lb) cooking apples (when peeled
and cored), 70ml (⅛ pint) water, juice and grated rind 1
lemon, 680g (1½lb) sugar.*

Rough chop peeled and cored apples, put in pan with water
and grated lemon rind; simmer till tender; add lemon juice and
mashed bananas; cook for 5 min, add sugar, stirring till dissolved;
boil rapidly to set.

Banana and Date Chutney *see under Date.*

BANANA AND LEMON JAM

6 bananas, 3 lemons, 450g (1lb) sugar.

Peel and slice bananas, grate lemon rind; squeeze and strain lemon juice; put bananas, rind and lemon juice into pan, cover with sugar; stand for 1 h; bring *very* slowly to boil (this will take about 1 h) then boil till set.

BANANA AND ORANGE JAM

Follow recipe above substituting 3 oranges for the lemons.

BANANA AND PINEAPPLE JAM

5 ripe bananas, 1 large tin pineapple pieces, 1.5 kg (3¼lb) sugar, 1 bottle commercial pectin.

Peel and thoroughly mash bananas; put in pan with pineapple pieces and their juice; add sugar; stir over low heat till sugar dissolved; bring quickly to boil, fast boiling for 1 min; remove from heat, add pectin, stir well and skim as necessary; pot and cover hot.

BARBERRY JELLY (1)

910 g (2lb) berries, 570ml (1 pint) water, juice ½ lemon, sugar.

Wash berries, put in pan with water, cook slowly till tender; strain through jelly bag; return to pan allowing 800g sugar per litre juice (1lb per pint), stirring till dissolved; bring slowly to boil, add lemon juice; boil fast to set.

BARBERRY JELLY (2)

910g (2lb) berries, 285ml (½ pint) water, juice ½ lemon, sugar.

Wash berries, put in fireproof dish in moderate oven till juice is running; add water, simmer 15 min; strain through jelly bag and continue as above. (A small quantity of mixed spice added to this jelly makes an ideal accompaniment to meat and game.)

BASIL JELLY

12 sprigs basil, 425ml (¾ pint) apple juice, 225g (½lb) sugar, 2tbs. lemon juice.

Put juices in pan, bring to boil; add sugar, stirring till dissolved; add basil sprigs; boil to set; strain and pot, add 2 or 3 basil leaves to each jar when cool.

BEAN CHUTNEY (GREEN BEANS)

450g (1lb) runner or dwarf beans, 450g (1lb) brown sugar, 2 large onions, 850ml (1½ pints) vinegar, 3 tsp. each turmeric and mustard, 1tsp. cornflour.

String and slice beans; boil till tender in salted water; strain well; put in pan with 710ml (1¼ pints) vinegar, chopped or sliced onions and sugar; boil 15 min; mix spices with remaining vinegar and cornflour, add to beans; boil further 15 min.

BEANS (Dried)

Use only young tender runner or dwarf beans; top, tail and string if necessary; cut in 50mm (2 in) lengths; blanch in boiling water for 2 min; drain thoroughly; spread out on flat containers and leave in sun or cooling oven with door slightly ajar; when they are brittle enough to break easily they can be stored in tins or jars, or even paper bags in a dark cupboard; the drying may be done over a period of days without detriment to the beans.

BEANS PICKLED (1)

French or dwarf beans, vinegar, brown sugar, allspice, salt, pepper.

Top, tail and string beans; halve if long; put in boiling salted water and boil till just tender; drain well; put in pan with vinegar to cover and 1.6kg sugar, 2tsp. allspice, salt and pepper to taste per litre vinegar (2lb per pint); boil all together for 5 min; remove beans to jar, pour over vinegar; cover whilst hot.

BEANS PICKLED (2)

450g (1lb) firm young green beans, 285ml (½ pint) boiling water, 285ml (½ pint) cider vinegar [or 150ml (¼ pint) vinegar, 150ml (¼ pint) dry cider], 113g (¼lb) brown sugar, tsp. salt, 113g (¼lb) small white onions (or shallots), dsp. dill seed, ¼tsp. each red pepper and turmeric.

Top and tail beans; put whole in salted boiling water; cook till crisp tender; drain well, pack in jars; put all other ingredients in pan, boil 3 min; pour over beans, seal airtight; do not use for six weeks.

BEANS PICKLED (3) (1799)

Pour boiling hot wine over your French beans and cover them close. Next day drain and dry them. Then pour over them boiling hot pickle of white wine vinegar, Jamaica pepper, black pepper, a little mace and ginger; repeat this for two or three days or till the beans look green then tie down.

BEANS SALTED

Green beans. Coarse salt (not refined salt)

Top and tail beans, slice or cut in lengths; young dwarf beans can be left whole; take large container (not metal), cover bottom with thick layer of salt, then good layer of beans, layer of salt, etc., continuing to the top of the vessel, finishing with salt; cover with weighted lid; at the end of a week, check container, fill with more beans and salt; continue this till container is solid packed; cover closely. (Rinse and soak beans before cooking in unsalted fast boiling water.)

BEETROOT CHUTNEY

1.4kg (3lb) beetroot, 225g (½lb) brown sugar, 680g (1½lb)
apples, 2 Spanish onions, 570ml (1 pint) vinegar,
juice 1 lemon, 1tsp. salt and ground ginger.

Boil beetroot for approx. 2 h according to size; when cold, peel and cut in cubes; peel, core and rough chop apples; rough chop onions; put apples, onions and all other ingredients (except beet) in pan; simmer about 1 h or till tender, stirring from time to time; add beet, boil further 15 mins.

BEETROOT PICKLED

Beetroot, spiced vinegar (see vinegars).

Wash beetroot without breaking skins; boil about 2 h (according to size); peel, slice, pack into jars; when cold cover with cold spiced vinegar; for good keeping do not pack jars too tightly.

BEETROOT RELISH

450g (1lb) cooked beetroot, 450g (1lb) uncooked chopped
cabbage, 225g (½lb) sugar, 2tbs. fresh grated horseradish
(dried can be used), 1tbs. mustard, 1tsp. salt, ½tsp. white
pepper, 570ml (1 pint) vinegar.

Chop beetroot roughly and cabbage very finely, put together in pan with all ingredients; cook for 30 min; pot and cover at once. (Incidentally this goes very well with fish.)

Beetroot and Blackberry Chutney *see under Blackberry.*

BENGAL CHUTNEY

15 large sour apples, 225g (½lb) onion, 450g (1lb) Demerara sugar, 225g (½lb) stoned raisins, 113g (¼lb) garlic, 1.7l (3 pints) vinegar, 56g (2oz) each mustard seed and ground ginger.

Bake apples to pulp; remove skins and cores; boil onions till tender in a little water; peel, slice and boil garlic and skim; put all ingredients in one pan, boil 15 min; pot and cover immediately. (This will keep 2–3 years and improves greatly with maturity.)

BILBERRY JAM

1.4kg (3lb) bilberries, 225g (½lb) rhubarb, 1.4kg (3lb) sugar.

Trim and cut rhubarb; put in pan with sugar, stirring till it boils, then boil rapidly for 10 min; add bilberries, stir till boiling then simmer gently to set, skimming as necessary.

BLACKBERRY CHEESE

910g (2lb) blackberries, 450g (1lb) cooking apples (unpeeled), 285ml (½ pint) water, sugar.

Chop apples, put in pan with blackberries and water; simmer till soft; put through liquidizer and/or sieve; return pulp to pan with 1kg sugar per kilogram pulp (1lb sugar per lb pulp), stirring till dissolved; boil rapidly to set. (You can use the blackberry pulp from Blackberry Jelly by simmering the apples till tender, add blackberry pulp with a little more water then liquidize, etc.)

BLACKBERRY CHUTNEY

*1.4kg (3lb) blackberries, 450g (1lb) cooking apples, 340g
(12oz) onions, 450g (1lb) brown sugar, 570ml (1 pint) white
vinegar, 3tsp. salt, 2tsp. ground ginger, 1tsp. mace, 14g (½oz)
mustard.*

Peel, core and rough chop apples, rough chop onions; put in pan
with blackberries and vinegar with spices; cook for 1 h simmering
gently (if you don't like pips, sieve at this stage); add sugar, bring
to boil stirring till dissolved, then cook till thick; pot and cover at
once.

BLACKBERRY CURD

*340g (¾lb) blackberries, 113g (¼lb) cooking apples,
340g (¾lb) butter, 450g (1lb) sugar, 1 lemon, 4 eggs.*

Wash blackberries, peel, core and chop apples, put in pan (without
water) on very gentle heat to draw juice and until fruit is tender
(this can be done in fireproof dish in very slow oven); put through
liquidizer and/or sieve; put into double saucepan, or bowl over
boiling water; add strained lemon juice, butter and sugar, stirring
constantly till sugar is melted; beat eggs, add to mixture; cook
slowly, stirring, till mixture thickens.

BLACKBERRY JAM

910g (2lb) blackberries, 450g (1lb) sugar, 2 lemons.

Husk and pick over fruit carefully; lay on large dish, cover with
sugar and juice of lemons; stand overnight; put into pan on gentle
heat, stirring till sugar dissolved, then boil for 45 min, or to set.

BLACKBERRY JELLY

450g (1lb) blackberries, 1 medium-sized cooking apple or juice of 1 lemon, 70ml (⅛ pint) water, sugar.

Rough chop apple and put in pan with blackberries and water; simmer till tender; strain through jelly bag; return to pan, adding 800g sugar per litre juice (1lb per pint), stirring till dissolved, then add lemon if used; boil rapidly to set.

BLACKBERRY JELLY SPICED

Follow recipe above, adding 1tsp. mixed spice with each 800g (1lb) sugar.

BLACKBERRY PICKLE

680g (1½lb) blackberries, 570ml (1 pint) white vinegar, 910g (2lb) sugar, 42g (1½oz) allspice, 14g (½oz) ground ginger.

Husk and wash berries, put in bowl, cover with sugar; stand overnight; put vinegar in pan, bring to boil; add berries, boil gently 30 min; add allspice and ginger, mix well, simmer further 5 min; pot and cover when cold.

BLACKBERRIES SPICED

1.1kg (2½lb) blackberries, 450g (1lb) sugar, 285ml (½ pint) spiced vinegar, 2 leaves rose geranium.

Put spiced vinegar in pan with sugar, simmer till dissolved; add berries, simmer 5 min or till tender; transfer fruit to jars; boil vinegar rapidly till syrupy; add geranium leaves to fruit; pour over fruit and cover closely while still hot.

BLACKBERRY AND APPLE CHUTNEY

Follow recipe for Blackberry Chutney, using 910g (2lb*)* black-berries and 910g (2lb) apples, instead of 1.4kg (3lb) blackberries and 450g (1lb) apples.

BLACKBERRY AND APPLE JAM

450g (1lb) blackberries, 450g (1lb) cooking apples (when peeled and cored), 910g (2lb) sugar, 70ml (⅛ pint) water.

Slice apples, put in pan with water, simmer till tender; add ber-ries, simmer further 10 min or till soft; add sugar stirring till dis-solved, then boil fast to set.

BLACKBERRY AND APPLE JELLY (1)

*1.4kg (3lb) blackberries, 450g (1lb) apples,
225g (½lb) caster sugar, preserving sugar, water.*

Husk berries, rough chop apples, put both in large bowl with caster sugar and 570ml (1 pint) water; stand in very slow oven till apples are stewed and juice of berries runs (this can be done in covered pan on a very low heat on the stove with a heat diffuser under the pan); strain through jelly bag; put juice in pan with 600g preserving sugar per litre juice, stirring till sugar dissolved; boil about ¾ h stirring frequently, skimming as necessary; pot and cover when cold.

BLACKBERRY AND APPLE JELLY (2)

*910g (2lb) blackberries, 910g (2lb) cooking apples,
1.7l (3 pints) water, sugar.*

Wash and rough chop apples; put in pan with berries and water; simmer to soft pulp; strain through jelly bag; put juice in pan with

800g sugar per litre juice (1lb per pint), stirring till dissolved; bring to boil, cook about 25 min or to set; pot and cover when cold. (The pulp from either of these recipes can be used for a cheese, or even a curd.)

BLACKBERRY AND BEETROOT CHUTNEY

450g (1lb) blackberries, 450g (1lb) cooked beetroot, 113g (4oz) apples (when peeled and cored), 113g (4oz) onions, 56g (2oz) sugar, 56g (2oz) sultanas, 70ml (⅛ pint) vinegar, 1tsp. each curry powder and ground ginger; mustard and cayenne, 6 peppercorns.

Wash, husk and drain berries; rough chop beetroot and apples, finely chop onions; put in pan with all other ingredients except mustard and cayenne; simmer till thickening; then add mustard and cayenne to taste; cook till thick; pot and cover when cold.

BLACKBERRY AND ELDERBERRY JAM

450g (1lb) blackberries, 450g (1lb) elderberries, 450g (1lb) sugar.

Stalk and husk fruit, put in pan, bruising slightly; heat very gently for about 25 min; warm sugar in oven and when quite hot add to fruit; bring to boil, cook 10 min or to set; pot and cover hot.

BLACKBERRY AND GOOSEBERRY JELLY

910g (2lb) blackberries, 450g (1lb) gooseberries, 285ml (½ pint) water, sugar.

Simmer fruits in water till completely soft; strain through jelly bag; put juice in pan with 800g sugar per litre liquid (1lb per pint), stirring till dissolved, then boil rapidly to set.

Blackberry and Marrow Chutney *see under Marrow.*

BLACKBERRY AND MARROW JAM

910g (2lb) blackberries, 910g (2lb) marrow (when peeled and seeded); 1.4kg (3lb) sugar, juice and rind of 2 small lemons, 285ml (½ pint) water.

Dice marrow and put in pan with berries and water; peel lemon and put in muslin bag; add to pan with strained juice of lemon; simmer till fruit and marrow are tender; remove muslin bag; add sugar, stirring till dissolved; then boil fast for 10 min.

BLACKBERRY AND PINEAPPLE JAM

450g (1lb) blackberries, 450g (1lb) fresh pineapple (when peeled), 2 large cooking apples, 1.4kg (3lb) sugar, juice 3 lemons, water.

Peel, core and slice apples, cube pineapple; put together in pan with minimum water; simmer 15 min; add berries, cook further 10 min or till soft; add sugar and lemon juice, stirring till sugar dissolved, then boil rapidly to set.

BLACKBERRY AND ROSEHIP JAM

1.4kg (3lb) blackberries, 450g (1lb) rosehips, sugar, water.

Chop rosehips finely, remove seeds, put in bowl, just cover with water; leave for 2 days; husk, wash and drain berries, add to rosehips; put bowl in warm oven till juice is running freely; transfer to pan, adding 1kg sugar per kilogram of fruit and liquid (1lb per pint), stirring over very low heat till sugar dissolves; bring to boil and boil rapidly to set, skimming as required.

Blackberries *see also Hedgerow Jam, Mixed Fruit Jam.*

BLACKCURRANT CHEESE

Blackcurrants, sugar, water.

Put currants in pan with 625ml water per kilogram fruit (½ pint per lb); simmer till tender; liquidize and/or sieve; return to pan with ¾kg sugar per kilogram pulp (¾lb per lb), stirring till sugar dissolved; simmer gently, stirring occasionally till purée thickens. [If you prefer a sweeter taste, allow 1kg per kilogram pulp (1lb sugar per lb).]

BLACKCURRANT JAM (1)

450g (1lb) blackcurrants, 570ml (1 pint) water, 680g (1½lb) sugar.

Stalk currants and wash well; put in pan with water; boil fairly fast for 30 min; add sugar, stirring till dissolved, then boil again for 10 min or to set.

BLACKCURRANT JAM (2)

450g (1lb) blackcurrants, 56g (2oz) rhubarb, 450g (1lb) sugar, 150ml (¼ pint) water.

Stalk and wash berries; cut rhubarb very finely; put all ingredients in pan, heating very gently and stirring constantly till sugar is dissolved; then boil steadily for about 45 min or to set. (There are many variations in quantities and method for blackcurrant jam, but I have found these two the simplest and most effective.)

BLACKCURRANT JELLY

Blackcurrants, sugar, water.

Stalk and wash currants, put in pan with water to cover; simmer till quite tender; strain through jelly bag; put juice in pan with 600g sugar per litre liquid (¾lb per pint), stirring till dissolved; boil to set.

BLACKCURRANT AND APPLE JAM

450g (1lb) currants, 450g (1lb) apples (when peeled and cored), 1.1kg (2½lb) sugar, 285ml (½ pint) water.

Stalk and wash currants, put in pan with water, simmer 15 min; add sliced apple; cook till soft; add sugar, stirring till dissolved, then boil rapidly to set.

BLACKCURRANT AND CHERRY JAM

910g (2lb) blackcurrants, 910g (2lb) stoned cherries (black for preference), 1.4kg (3lb) sugar, 570ml (1 pint) water.

Wash currants, put in pan with water, simmer gently for about 1 h; strain through jelly bag; put juice in pan, add cherries, simmer 20 min, add sugar, stirring till dissolved; bring to boil, simmer 10 min or to set.

Blackcurrant and Gooseberry Jam; Blackcurrant and Gooseberry Jelly *see under Gooseberry.*
Blackcurrant and Loganberry Jam; Blackcurrant and Loganberry Jelly *see under Loganberry.*

BLACKCURRANT AND PINEAPPLE JAM

450g (1lb) currants, 450g (1lb) pineapple (when peeled),
910g (2lb) sugar, 1 orange.

Stalk and wash currants and put in pan with rough chopped pineapple; simmer very gently together till tender; add grated rind of orange and sugar, stirring till dissolved; bring to gentle boil and cook till thick. (This can be made with tinned fruit using ½ bottle commerical pectin – it is delicious with hot puddings in the winter.)

Blackcurrant and Raspberry Jam; Blackcurrant and Raspberry Jelly *see under Raspberry.*

BLACKCURRANT AND REDCURRANT JAM

450g (1lb) blackcurrants, 450g (1lb) redcurrants,
910g (2lb) sugar, 425ml (¾ pint) water.

Stalk and wash currants, put in pan with water, simmer till very soft; add sugar, stirring till dissolved, then boil rapidly to set. (This jam sets very quickly.)

BLACKCURRANT AND REDCURRANT JELLY

450g (1lb) blackcurrants, 450g (1lb) redcurrants,
water, sugar.

Stalk and wash currants and put in pan with 570ml (1 pint) water; simmer gently till thoroughly tender; strain through jelly bag; put juice in pan with 800g sugar for each litre (1lb per pint) liquid stirring till dissolved; bring to fast boil, cook to set.

BLACKCURRANT AND RHUBARB JAM (1)

Rhubarb, blackcurrants, sugar, water.

Chop rhubarb and stew in little water till tender; strain through jelly bag; for each 570ml (1 pint) of juice add 1.4kg (3lb) washed and stalked currants and simmer till tender; add 1.4kg (3lb) sugar for each 1.4kg (3lb) currants, stirring till dissolved, then boil to set; pot and cover immediately. (If the currant skins seem tough add about 28g (1oz) butter to jam whilst boiling.)

BLACKCURRANT AND RHUBARB JAM (2)

450g (1lb) blackcurrants, 450g (1lb) rhubarb, 910g (2lb) sugar, 285ml (½ pint) water.

Stalk and wash currants and simmer 15 min in water; add chopped rhubarb; cook till soft; add sugar stirring till dissolved; boil rapidly to set.

Blackcurrants *see also Tutti Frutti Jam, Wine Jelly.*
Blaeberry, Blueberry *see Bilberry.*
Bramble *see Blackberry.*

C

Calamondin Preserve *see Kumquat Preserve.*

CAPERS PICKLED

Capers, water, coarse salt, spiced white vinegar (see vinegars).

Make brine of 100g salt to 1l water (2oz to 1 pint) and soak capers for 24 h; drain well; put in jars, cover with spiced vinegar and close down.

CARROT CHUTNEY

450g (1lb) carrots, 84g (3oz) brown sugar, 56g (2oz) sultanas, 570ml (1 pint) vinegar, 1tsp. ground ginger and mixed spice, 12 peppercorns, bay leaf.

Wash, scrape and grate or rough chop carrots; put in pan with all ingredients; simmer till tender, stirring occasionally, and liquid is syrupy.

CARROT JAM

Carrots, sugar, lemon, sweet almonds, cooking brandy.

Wash, scrape and small chop carrots; cook in small quantity of water till quite tender; liquidize or sieve, put purée in pan with 450g (1lb) sugar, grated rind and juice of 2 lemons per 570ml (1 pint) purée; stirring till sugar dissolves; then boil to set; add 14g (½oz) finely shredded blanched almonds and 1tbs. brandy for each 450g (1lb) sugar, stirring in well; pot and cover. (NB. This jam will not keep without the brandy.)

CARROT MARMALADE

*910g (2lb) carrots, 910g (2lb) sugar, 3 lemons,
570ml (1 pint) water.*

Squeeze juice from lemons; shred peel and tie in muslin bag with pips, and put all in bowl with water; stand overnight; clean, scrape and dice carrots; put in pan with lemon and cook till tender; add sugar, stirring till dissolved; remove muslin bag; boil rapidly to set.

CARROTS SPICED

*12 medium cooked carrots, 285ml (½ pint) vinegar, 285ml
(½ pint) water, 6 cloves, tsp. cinnamon, tsp. salt.*

Pack carrots into jars (if liked they can be quartered lengthwise); boil together vinegar, water, salt, cinnamon and cloves; strain and when cold pour over carrots to cover, then tie down; leave at least 2 weeks before use.

CARROT, APPLE AND PEACH MARMALADE

*450g (1lb) diced carrots, 450g (1lb) peeled, cored and diced
cooking apples, 225g (½lb) diced peaches, juice 1 lemon,
680g (1½lb) sugar.*

Put all ingredients in pan and boil rapidly till clear.

CAULIFLOWER PICKLED

Sound cauliflowers, salt, water, spiced white vinegar
(see Vinegars).

Break cauliflower heads into small pieces; put in brine of 100g
salt to 1l water (2oz per pint); stand overnight; drain thoroughly,
pack into jars and completely cover with cold spiced vinegar.

CAULIFLOWER, SWEET PICKLED

As above, adding 2tsp. sugar to each litre vinegar (½ pint).

Cauliflower *see also Mixed Pickle, Piccalilli.*

CHERRY CHUTNEY

680g (1½lb) cherries, 340g (¾lb) cooking apples, 570ml
(1 pint) vinegar, 225g (½lb) onions, 2tsp. salt, 1tsp. ground
ginger, 225g (½lb) sugar, 14g (½oz) pickling spice,
225g (8oz) chopped nuts (if liked).

Simmer cherries in 285ml (½ pint) vinegar till tender and remove
stones; return to pan with rough chopped apples and onions, ginger, salt and pickling spices (in muslin bag); cook till fruit is soft,

add remaining vinegar and sugar, stirring till dissolved, then boil steadily till thick; if nuts are liked, add at this stage, then pot and cover. (A tart cherry, like a Morello, is best for this.)

CHERRY CONSERVE

450g (1lb) cherries, 340g (12oz) sugar, juice of ½ lemon, 56g (2oz) raisins, 56g (2oz) chopped walnuts.

Stone cherries and put in pan with raisins, with the cherry stones in muslin bag; cook very slowly till soft; add lemon juice and sugar and stir till dissolved, then boil rapidly to set; stir in chopped walnuts; pot and cover.

CHERRY JAM (1)

450g (1lb) stoned Morello cherries, 680g (1½lb) sugar, 570ml (1 pint) fruit juice (apple, rhubarb or gooseberry).

Put cherries and fruit juice in pan, bring to boil; simmer 10 min; add sugar, stirring till dissolved; boil, still stirring, till fruit is tender and syrup jellies; pot and cover hot.

CHERRY JAM (2)

450g (1lb) stoned cherries, 340g (¾lb) sugar, juice ½ lemon.

Put cherries in pan, with stones in muslin bag, and simmer till soft (if cherries are very firm, put a little water with them); add lemon juice and sugar, stirring till dissolved; boil rapidly to set.

CHERRY JELLY

Cherries, apple juice, sugar, water.

Put cherries in pan with water just to cover; simmer till completely tender; strain through jelly bag; return juice to pan with ½ litre apple juice and 800g sugar to each litre cherry juice (1lb per pint); stir till sugar is dissolved then boil rapidly to set; allow to cool slightly before potting and leave 24 h before covering.

CHERRIES PICKLED (1)

910g (2lb) sour red cherries, 340g (¾lb) Demerara sugar, 285ml (½ pint) cider vinegar [or 150ml (¼ pint) each white vinegar and dry cider], 3 x 10cm (4in) sticks cinnamon, 1tsp. whole cloves.

Tie spices in muslin bag and put in pan with vinegar and sugar; boil 4 min; add cherries, cook 15 min; remove cherries to jar; return liquid to boil, and boil fast till syrupy; pour over cherries to cover and seal tightly.

CHERRIES PICKLED (2)

Cherries, sugar, crushed cinnamon sticks, cloves, white wine vinegar.

Prick cherries lightly with needle, put layer in a wide-necked jar, scatter some sugar, a few flakes of cinnamon and a couple of cloves, and continue in layers till jar is full; boil vinegar and allow to become cold; pour very slowly over cherries and slightly 'rattle' jar to ensure there are no air-holes; cover very tightly; leave in warmish place for three days before storing normally.

CHERRIES PRESERVED

Cherries, caster sugar, water.

Make a thick syrup of 400g sugar to 1 litre water (½lb per pint); stone cherries, put in pan with syrup, bring to boil; transfer to china or earthenware bowl; stand for 3 days; drain syrup into pan, boil again, pour over cherries; stand 24 h; drain, and put cherries on fine sieve, leaving until completely dry; store in air-tight container. (Use syrup to make a jelly, or with other cherries for a pie or flan.)

CHERRY AND APPLE JAM

910g (2lb) ripe cherries, 450g (1lb) apples (when peeled and cored), 1.4kg (3lb) sugar, 150ml (¼ pint) water.

Slice apples and simmer slowly in water till soft; slit cherries, add to apples and cook till softened; add sugar stirring till dissolved, bring to fast boil, cook to set, removing cherry stones as they rise.

Cherry and Apricot Jam *see under Apricot.*
Cherry and Blackcurrant Jam *see under Blackcurrant.*
Cherry and Gooseberry Jam *see under Gooseberry.*
Cherry and Loganberry Jam *see under Loganberry.*

CHERRY AND PINEAPPLE PRESERVE

*1.4kg (3lb) sharp cherries, small pineapple,
1.1kg (2½lb) sugar, water.*

Wash cherries, slit and put in pan; peel and shred pineapple and add to cherries with very small quantity of water; simmer very slowly till fruit is tender; add sugar, stirring till dissolved, then boil fast for 20 min or to set, removing cherry stones as they rise to surface.

CHERRY AND REDCURRANT JAM

910g (2lb) stoned cherries, 910g (2lb) redcurrants,
1.4kg (3lb) sugar, 570ml (1 pint) water.

Wash redcurrants, put in pan with water; simmer approx. 1 h till soft; strain through jelly bag; put cherries in pan with redcurrant juice; simmer 20 min, then add sugar, stirring till dissolved; then boil till set.

CHERRY JAM (Black Cherries)

Follow recipe for Morello cherry jam, but use only half the quantity of lemon juice.

CHERRY JAM (Wild Cherries)

1.4kg (3lb) wild cherries, 450g (1lb) sugar,
570ml (1 pint) gooseberry or currant juice.

Slit cherries, put in pan, just cover with water; boil till water nearly evaporated, removing stones as they rise; add sugar and fruit juice, boil rapidly to set (approx. 30 min), stirring continuously and skimming as necessary; remove any remaining stones before potting.

CHERRY PRESERVE (Black Cherries)

680g (1½lb) black cherries, 450g (1lb) sugar, juice 1 lemon.

Put cherries into bowl, sprinkle with sugar and leave overnight; put into pan with lemon juice, heating very gently till sugar is dissolved, stirring constantly; boil rapidly till syrup thickens.

CHESTNUT JAM

910g (2lb) chestnuts, 680g (1½lb) loaf sugar, 285ml (½ pint) water, 2tsp. vanilla essence.

Cut chestnuts top and bottom; boil till tender; peel and skin; liquidize or crush through coarse sieve; make a syrup of the water, sugar and essence, add chestnuts; cook to a firm consistency. (Absolutely dry storage is essential and it is not a long-keeping jam, but fun for Christmas.)

CHILLI SAUCE

3 red peppers, 910g (2lb) ripe tomatoes, 2 onions, 113g (¼lb) sugar, 1.1l (2 pints) vinegar, 2tbs. salt and ground ginger, 1tbs. cloves, allspice, cinnamon, mustard and celery seed.

Dip tomatoes in boiling water and peel; put in pan with finely chopped or rough minced peppers and onion and all other ingredients; bring to boil, then boil slowly for about 2 h until thick, stirring frequently.

CHILLIES PICKLED

Firm bright chillies (red or green), spiced white vinegar.

Remove stalks from chillies, slice carefully lengthwise and remove seeds, leaving chilli whole; pack neatly into jars, cover with spiced white vinegar and seal down.

Cider Apple Butter *see Apple Butter, American.*

CLEMENTINE MARMALADE

450g (1lb) clementines, 850ml (1½ pints) water, 680g (1½lb) sugar, tsp. lemon juice.

Slice clementines finely, putting pips in muslin bag; soak fruit and pips overnight in water; put in pan, simmer 1½ h or till tender; remove muslin bag; add sugar (preferably warmed) and lemon juice, stirring till sugar is dissolved; boil rapidly to set, approx. 20 min.

Clove and Apple Jam *see under Apple.*

COCONUT JAM

Coconut, sugar, vanilla essence.

Drain coconut, break open and grate or cut flesh very thinly; weigh: put in pan equal quantity of sugar and very small quantity of water, stirring over very low heat till dissolved; bring to boil, add coconut and 6 drops vanilla essence for each kilogram (3 drops per lb); cook very slowly, stirring often, for about 1½ h.

CORN RELISH

5 cobs corn, 570ml (1 pint) vinegar, 113g (¼lb) sugar,
2tsp. salt, 3tsp. dry mustard, ½tsp. turmeric, ¼ small firm
cabbage, 1 onion, 2 small red and 1 green pepper.

Cook cobs in boiling water for 2 min, rinse in cold water; remove grains; put vinegar, sugar, salt and spices in pan, bring to boil; add finely chopped cabbage and onion, and seeded and chopped peppers, together with grains of corn; boil gently till vegetables are tender, stirring constantly.

CRABAPPLE BUTTER

910g (2lb) crabapples, 285ml (½ pint) water, sugar.

Quarter crabapples, put in pan with water and cook till really soft; put through liquidizer and/or sieve; return to pan allowing 500g sugar for each kilogram pulp (½lb per lb); cook till thick, stirring constantly.

CRABAPPLE JELLY

Crabapples, water, lemon juice, cloves, sugar.

Halve apples, put in pan with 1.25l water for each kilogram fruit (1 pint per lb), simmer till tender; strain through jelly bag; put juice in pan with 6 cloves, 2tbs. lemon juice and 800g sugar per

litre juice (3 cloves, 1tbs. lemon juice, 1lb sugar per pint), stirring
till sugar is dissolved; boil gently to set; pot, cover when cold.

Crabapples *see also Apples spiced, Apple Struper, Hedgerow Jam or
as a variation of apple recipes.*

CRANBERRY CHEESE

*450g (1lb) cranberries, 56g (2oz) seedless raisins, 285ml (½
pint) water, 340g (¾lb) sugar, 1 orange, 56g (2oz) chopped
walnuts.*

Simmer cranberries till soft; liquidize and/or sieve; add sugar,
raisins and walnuts; bring slowly to boil, stirring constantly; add
thinly sliced orange (discard pips), simmer further 20 min.

CRANBERRY CHUTNEY

*450g (1lb) cranberries, 450g (1lb) apples, 225g (½lb) sugar,
170g (6oz) raisins, 285ml (½ pint) vinegar, 2tsp. pickling
spice (in muslin bag), 1tsp. each salt and mixed spice.*

Peel, core and chop apples; put in pan with half the vinegar; add
all other ingredients except sugar; simmer till fruit is soft; add
remaining vinegar and sugar, stirring till dissolved; boil slowly till
thick, remove muslin bag before potting.

Cranberry Conserve *see Cranberry Cheese.*

CRANBERRY JAM

450g (1lb) cranberries, 910g (2lb) sugar,
150ml (¼ pint) water.

Rinse berries several times; put in pan with water and sugar, stirring till sugar is dissolved; boil rapidly to set. [56g (2oz) chopped apple and ½tsp. cinnamon may be added during cooking for an alternative flavour.]

CRANBERRY JELLY

910g (2lb) cranberries, 425ml (¾ pint) water, sugar.

Simmer cranberries in water till tender; strain through jelly bag; put juice in pan with 800g sugar per little liquid (1lb per pint), stirring till dissolved; boil rapidly to set.

CRANBERRY KETCHUP

450g (1lb) cranberries, 340g (¾lb) sugar, 150ml (¼ pint)
vinegar, 225g (½lb) brown sugar, 1tsp. allspice, ½tsp.
cinnamon and ground clove.

Put fruit, water, vinegar and spices in pan and cook till fruit is tender; add both sugars, stirring till dissolved, boil fast for 5 min, bottle and cover tightly whilst hot.

CRANBERRY SAUCE

450g (1lb) cranberries, 225g (½lb) sugar, grated rind 1 lemon,
285ml (½ pint) water.

Bring sugar and water to boil, stirring till sugar dissolved; add fruit; simmer to a pulp; liquidize and/or sieve; return to pan, add grated rind of lemon, boil slowly for 10 min; pot and cover hot. (Add a little sherry or port before bottling if liked; and for a thicker sauce, add a little arrowroot with the last cooking).

CRANBERRY AND APPLE JELLY

Follow recipe for Apple Jelly using 1kg cranberries for each 1½kg apples (1lb per lb).

CRANBERRY AND APPLE SAUCE

225g (½lb) cranberries, 225g (½lb) apples (peeled and cored), 56g (2oz) sugar, 28g (1oz) butter, 150ml (¼ pint) water.

Slice apples finely, put in pan with cranberries and water; simmer very slowly to a pulp; liquidize and/or sieve; put in pan with butter and sugar and simmer gently, stirring, for 10 min; beat well with wooden spoon, pot and cover.

Cranberry, Apple and Quince Jelly *see Paradise Jelly*.

CRANBERRY AND GRAPE JELLY

450g (1lb) cranberries, 450g (1lb) white grapes, 150ml (¼ pint) water, sugar, lemon juice.

Simmer fruit in water till soft; strain through jelly bag; put juice in pan with juice of 2 lemons and 800g sugar per litre liquid (juice 1 lemon and 1lb sugar per pint), stirring till dissolved; boil rapidly to set.

CRANBERRY ORANGE CONSERVE

450g (1lb) cranberries, 1 orange, 56g (2oz) stoned raisins, 56g (2oz) walnuts, 340g (¾lb) sugar 285ml (½ pint) water.

Wash fruit, finely slice orange, discarding pips; pick over cranberries and put in pan with orange and water; simmer till tender; add raisins, walnuts and sugar, stirring till dissolved; bring to boil, simmer 20 min or to set; pot and cover immediately.

CRANBERRY AND ORANGE RELISH

450g (1lb) cranberries, 1large orange, 225g (½lb) sugar.

Cut orange, remove pips, and put through mincer with cranberries; put in pan, add sugar, stirring till dissolved; bring to boil, simmer 10 min. (This relish can be potted without actual cooking for short-term use.)

Cranberry and Pumpkin Jam *see under Pumpkin.*
Cranberry and Quince Preserve *see under Quince.*

CRANBERRY AND RAISIN JAM

*450g (1lb) cranberries, 113g (¼lb) raisins,
150ml (¼ pint) water, 570 g (1¼lb) sugar.*

Proceed as for Cranberry Jam.

CUCUMBER JAM

1 cucumber, water, sugar, lemon juice.

Peel and dice cucumber and weigh; put in pan with *very* small quantity of water, simmer till just soft, then add juice of 2 lemons and 1kg sugar per kilogram cucumber (1 lemon and 1lb sugar per lb cucumber), stirring very gently till dissolved, then boil rapidly to set. (For a darker colouring add a few drops of green colouring.)

CUCUMBER JELLY

910g (2lb) whole cucumber, sugar, lemon,
ginger to taste, water.

Cut up cucumber, put in pan with *very* little water; simmer to soft pulp; strain through jelly bag; put juice in pan with 800g sugar, juice of 2 lemons and a pinch of ginger for each litre (1lb sugar, 1 lemon, pinch ginger per pint), stirring till sugar dissolved; boil rapidly to set.

CUCUMBER PICKLE

1.4kg (3lb) cucumber, 56g (2oz) salt, 2 onions, 1 green pep-
per, 42g (1½oz) mustard seed, 1tsp. celery seeds, ½ blade mace,
280g (10oz) sugar, 570ml (1 pint) white vinegar.

Wash cucumber, cut in small pieces (without peeling); put in bowl, cover with salt; stand overnight; peel and very finely slice onions; wash, halve, core and seed pepper and cut in strips; put vinegar in pan with spices (in muslin bag), onions, pepper and sugar; heat gently, stirring till sugar is dissolved; then boil rapidly 2 min with lid on; strain; drain cucumber, put in pan with strained vinegar; bring to boil, simmer 5 min.

CUCUMBER HOT PICKLE

Cucumbers, salt, cloves, peppercorns, horseradish, shallots, chillies, bay leaves, tarragon, root ginger, garlic (if liked), white vinegar.

Peel cucumber, cut in chunks; put in pan, just cover with water, adding 50g salt per litre water (1oz salt per pint); boil for 1 min; drain thoroughly; pack into jars, cover with vinegar; stand for 3 days, drain vinegar into pan; add ginger, cloves, peppercorns, bring to boil, add cucumber pieces for 1 min; remove carefully and put in jars with horseradish, shallots, cloves, bay leaves, chopped garlic and tarragon in odd places and 1 chilli per jar; strain vinegar and when cold fill jars; cover closely.

CUCUMBER PICKLED (1)

Cucumbers, vinegar, salt.

Peel cucumber, slice thinly; spread on dish, cover with salt, stand overnight; drain off well, pack into jars with alternate layers of salt; cover closely; when required, remove from jar, soak in cold water, drain well and serve with vinegar.

CUCUMBER PICKLED (2)

Cucumber, salt, spiced vinegar (see Vinegars)

Cut cucumber in 12mm (½in) slices; put in bowl, cover with salt; stand overnight; rinse well, drain thoroughly, pack into jars; cover with cold spiced white vinegar; seal down.

CUCUMBER PICKLED (3)

(A very tall jar, such as a glass sweet jar is needed.)
Whole cucumbers, salt, grated horseradish, shallots, capers, nut-
meg, cloves, sugar, mustard seed, white vinegar.

From each cucumber, cut triangular wedge the full length; remove seeds and soft pulp; make a mixture of equal quantities of fresh grated horseradish, finely minced shallots and capers, add small quantity sugar and mustard seed with clove and nutmeg to flavour; put cucumber and wedges on dish, scatter generously with coarse salt and leave overnight; drain well and dry, fill with spiced mixture, replace wedges and tie in place with fine string; pack cucumbers upright in jar and fill with cold white vinegar.

CUCUMBER SWEET PICKLED (1)

Use Cucumber Pickled recipe (2) adding 3½tsp. sugar per litre vinegar (2tsp. per pint).

CUCUMBER SWEET PICKLED (2)

Cucumbers, white vinegar, sugar, cinnamon, ginger, nutmeg.

Peel cucumbers, cut lengthwise, remove seeds, cut in 25mm (1in) pieces; put in bowl, cover with vinegar; stand 48 h; drain vinegar into pan with 130g sugar, ½tsp. cinnamon and ginger and a pinch of nutmeg per litre vinegar (½lb sugar, tsp. cinnamon and ginger, ¼tsp. nutmeg per 3 pints); boil 15 min; add cucumber, boil 2 min; put cucumber in jars, pour over hot vinegar, cover, stand for 2 weeks; drain off vinegar, boil up again and when cold pour over cucumber; seal tightly.

CUCUMBERS PRESERVED

Small half-grown cucumbers, sugar, lemon, root ginger, water.

Throw cucumbers into pan of boiling water, scald for 3 min; remove and pierce with needle in 3–4 places; put on sieve to drain; for every 1kg weight cucumber allow 1kg sugar, 1.25l water, rind of 2 lemons and small piece of root ginger (for 1lb cucumber: 1lb sugar, 1 pint water, rind 1 lemon, piece root ginger); put all in pan with cucumbers, bring to boil, simmer gently 5 min; remove cucumbers carefully and pack in large jar, strain vinegar and pour over them; cover closely and stand for four days; drain liquid into pan, boil up again, strain once more and pour over cucumbers; cover closely; check jar from time to time and if any sign of froth or bubbles, drain liquid and boil again.

CUCUMBER AND GINGER JAM

Follow recipe for Cucumber Jam, adding ground ginger to personal taste.

CUCUMBER AND ONION PICKLE

2 cucumbers, 2 good-sized onions, salt, sugar, mustard seed, celery seed, curry powder, white vinegar, water.

Wash and slice cucumbers into 6mm (¼in) lengths; peel and slice onions very thinly; put in large bowl in layers, sprinkling liberally with coarse salt; stand overnight; put in pan 150ml (¼ pint) white vinegar, 150ml (¼ pint) water, 113g (¼lb) sugar, 1tsp. mustard seed, 1tsp. celery seed and ¼tsp. curry powder; bring to boil; drain cucumber and onion well, add to pan, simmer for 10 min; pot and close tightly.

Cucumber Vinegar *see Vinegars.*

D

DAMSON BUTTER

Damsons, sugar, water.

Wash fruit and slit sides; put in pan with very small quantity of water; simmer till tender; remove stones; liquidize and/or sieve; put purée in pan with 800g sugar per litre purée (1lb per pint), and stir over very low heat till sugar is dissolved; continue stirring until quite stiff; pot and cover immediately.

DAMSON CHUTNEY (1)

910g (2lb) damsons, 1 onion, 113g (¼lb) raisins, 56g (2oz) dates, 340g (¾lb) brown sugar, 570ml (1 pint) vinegar, 1tsp. salt, ¼tsp. allspice, 14g (½oz) ground ginger, small clove of garlic (if liked).

Wash and slit damsons, chop onion, raisins and dates; crush garlic (if used); put all ingredients in pan, simmer about 1½ h, removing stones as they rise; when thick pot, and cover when cold.

DAMSON CHUTNEY (2)

*680g (1½lb) damsons, 225g (½lb) onions, 340g (¾lb) cooking
apples (when peeled and cored), small piece bruised root ginger,
14g (½oz) pickling spice, 225g (½lb) sugar.*

Follow method above, tying ginger and spices in muslin bag,
which is removed before potting.

DAMSON JAM

910g (2lb) damsons, 570ml (1 pint) water, 1.4kg (3lb) sugar.

Wash and slit damsons; put in pan with water; simmer gently for
30 min or till tender; add sugar, stirring till dissolved; bring to
boil quickly; removing stones as they rise; boil fast to set. (There
are several variations of quantities for Damson Jam, but this is a
good basic recipe.)

DAMSON JELLY

Damsons, sugar, water.

Put fruit in pan, cover with water; simmer very slowly till tender;
strain through jelly bag; put juice in pan with 800g sugar for each
litre liquid (1lb per pint), stirring till dissolved; boil gently till set;
pot and cover when cold.

DAMSONS PICKLED

*910g (2lb) damsons, 285ml (½ pint) white vinegar, small stick
cinnamon, 1 blade mace, 2 cloves, 14g (½oz) allspice,
small piece root ginger, rind of ½ lemon.*

Wash and stalk fruit; chop lemon peel, tie spices in muslin bag,
and put all ingredients in pan; simmer till fruit is quite tender;

remove fruit carefully to jars; boil liquid till slightly thick; fill jars to cover fruit; close down tightly.

DAMSONS SWEET PICKLED

Follow recipe above allowing 1kg sugar for each 2 kg fruit (1lb per 2lb fruit).

DAMSON AND APPLE JAM

680g (1½lb) damsons, 450g (1lb) apples (peeled and cored), 285ml (½ pint) water, 910g (2lb) sugar.

Slit damsons, rough chop apples and put in pan with water; simmer slowly till soft; add sugar, stirring till dissolved; boil rapidly to set, removing stones as they rise.

DAMSON AND APPLE JELLY

450g (1lb) damsons, 450g (1lb) apples, 285ml (½ pint) water, sugar.

Put fruit in pan with water; simmer till soft, strain through jelly bag; put juice in pan with 800g sugar per litre liquid (1lb per pint), stir till dissolved, then boil rapidly to set.

DAMSON AND MARROW JAM

450g (1lb) damsons, 450g (1lb) marrow (when peeled and seeded), 150ml (¼ pint) water, 910g (2lb) sugar.

Slit damsons, put in pan with marrow (cut up) and water; simmer till tender, removing stones as they are released; add sugar, stirring till dissolved; boil rapidly to set, removing remaining stones as they rise.

DATE CHUTNEY

450g (1lb) stoned dates, 1 small onion, 425ml (¾ pint) cider vinegar (or mixture vinegar and dry cider), 1tsp. mixed spice, pinch cayenne pepper, salt to taste, ½tsp. minced garlic (if liked), or use garlic salt instead of plain salt.

Put cider vinegar, sugar and garlic (if used) into pan; simmer 10 min; add remaining ingredients; cook gently, stirring from time to time, till thickened; pot and seal hot.

DATE JAM

450g (1lb) stoned dates, 225g (½lb) sugar, 285ml (½ pint) water, grated rind and juice of 1 lemon.

Chop dates, put in pan with water; boil 30 min; add rind and juice of lemon and sugar, stirring till dissolved, then boil gently till thick.

DATE JAM (without sugar)

450g (1lb) stoned dates, 285ml (½ pint) water, 285ml (½ pint) lemon jelly, 1 lemon.

Chop dates, put in pan with water; simmer 1 h; add grated rind and juice of lemon, with the lemon jelly dissolved in boiling water; boil all together, stirring well; pot and cover hot.

DATE PICKLE

450g (1lb) stoned dates, 425ml (¾ pint) vinegar, 28g (1oz) pickling spice, salt.

Tie spices in muslin bag, put in pan with vinegar and pinch of salt; boil together for 10 min; remove from heat; stir in chopped dates; pot and cover; ready for use in 3 months.

DATE AND APPLE CHUTNEY (1)

225g (½lb) stoned dates, 680g (1½lb) apples (peeled and cored), 570ml (1 pint) vinegar, 225g (½lb) onions, 28g (1oz) ground ginger, pinch of cayenne and ground cloves.

Chop dates, apples, and onions and put in pan with all ingredients; simmer gently together for 1 h stirring from time to time, or till thickened; pot and cover cold.

DATE AND APPLE CHUTNEY (2)

450g (1lb) cooking dates, 450g (1lb) cooking apples, 1 clove garlic (if liked), 225g (½lb) currants, 225g (½lb) brown sugar, 285ml (½ pint) vinegar, 7g (¼oz) ground ginger, salt to taste.

Chop dates; peel, core and thinly slice apples; crush garlic with salt (do not use wooden spoon – the taste and smell will stay for ever!); put all ingredients in pan with a little more salt to taste; bring to boil, simmer 30 min or till thickened; pot and cover cold.

Date and Apple Preserve *see under Apple.*

DATE AND BANANA CHUTNEY

225g (½lb) dates, 6 bananas, 450g (1lb) onions, 285ml (½ pint) vinegar, 225g (½lb) treacle, 113g (¼lb) crystallized ginger or 2tsp. ground ginger, 1tsp. curry powder.

Chop dates and onions; peel and slice bananas; put in pan with vinegar; simmer till tender; add spices and treacle; cook gently till thick and dark brown in colour.

DATE AND FIG JAM

450g (1lb) stoned dates, 450g (1lb) dried figs, 1 packet orange jelly, 2 lemons, water.

Chop dates and figs into small pieces; put in pan with water and juice of lemons; simmer till soft; dissolve orange jelly in 285ml (½ pint) boiling water; add to pan, cook for further 10 min; pot and cover hot. (This is not a long-keeping jam.)

DATE AND LEMON CHUTNEY

340g (¾lb) stoned dates, 225g (½lb) onions, 225g (½lb) lemons, 113g (4oz) sultanas, 340g (¾lb) sugar, 113g (4oz) treacle, 28g (1oz) salt, 710ml (1¼ pints) vinegar, pinch of cayenne.

Grate rind of 1 lemon, remove pith, peel other lemons; slice all lemons, remove pips; fine chop (or mince) onions and dates; put vinegar, sugar, treacle, salt and cayenne in pan; bring to boil; add fruits; simmer about 45 min or till thick.

DATE AND ORANGE CHUTNEY

Follow recipe above, substituting oranges for lemons.

Dates *see also Fig Chutney.*

DRIED FRUIT PICKLE

225g (½lb) each prunes, dates, apricots and apples, 225g (½lb) sugar, 1.1l (2 pints) spiced vinegar (see Vinegars).

Soak fruits overnight in water; drain well; put in pan with very small quantity of water; simmer till tender; drain; put sugar and vinegar in pan; boil gently till syrupy; remove from heat, add fruits, stir all together well; pot and cover; do not use for at least 1 month. (You can use any variations of dried fruits for this recipe, according to personal likes and dislikes.)

DRYING FRUITS AND VEGETABLES *see page xxvii*

Only a few individual fruits and vegetables have been listed, but the basic principles are the same.

For vegetables follow 'Green beans, dried', cleaning, preparing and blanching before spreading on trays to dry. For fruits, cut in half, remove stones or cores, and dry face down. Apples are usually dried in rings, and do note that fruits such as apples and pears should be put in a bowl of salted water during preparation otherwise they will discolour quickly.

If the drying process has been done in a cool oven, never store away whilst still warm. Leave for 24 h or overnight, and pack into airtight containers when cold.

E

EGGS PICKLED

Eggs, spiced vinegar (see Vinegars).

Hard boil eggs, cool under running cold water tap; shell and remove inner skin; when completely cold, pack into glass jar; bring vinegar to boil, pour over eggs; tie down; leave for 3 days before use.

ELDERBERRY CHUTNEY

Follow Apple Chutney (4) using 450g (1lb) elderberries and 450g (1lb) apples instead of 910g (2lb) apples.

ELDERBERRY JAM

450g (1lb) elderberries, 450g (1lb) sugar, juice 1 lemon.

Wash fruit, put in pan, crush with wooden spoon; simmer till soft; add sugar, stirring till dissolved, then add lemon juice; boil rapidly to set.

ELDERBERRY JELLY

Follow recipe for Blackcurrant Jelly, adding juice of 2 lemons per litre fruit juice (1 lemon per pint).

ELDERBERRIES SPICED

910g (2lb) elderberries, 680g (1½lb) sugar, 150ml (¼ pint) vinegar, 150ml (¼ pint) water, 2 small sticks cinnamon, 14g (½oz.) each whole cloves and allspice.

Tie spices in muslin bag; put in pan with vinegar and water; bring to boil, then allow to cool; add berries, simmer till tender; add sugar, stirring till dissolved, simmer 10 min; transfer to bowl, cool quickly; leave overnight; remove spice bag; drain liquid into pan and put fruit in jars; bring liquid to boil, pour over berries; seal whilst hot.

ELDERBERRY AND APPLE JAM

450g (1lb) elderberries, 450g (1lb) apples (when peeled and cored), 910g (2lb) sugar, 285ml (½ pint) water.

Put fruit in pan with water; simmer till tender; add sugar, stirring till dissolved; boil fast to set.

ELDERBERRY AND APPLE JELLY

450g (1lb) elderberries, 450g (1lb) sweet apples, sugar, water.

Wash fruit, quarter apples without peeling or coring; put in pan with water just to cover; simmer till tender; add elderberries; simmer till tender; strain through jelly bag; put juice in pan with 600g sugar per litre liquid (¾lb per pint), stirring till dissolved; boil rapidly to set.

Elderberry and Blackberry Jam *see under Blackberry*.
Elderberry *see also Hedgerow Jam, Mixed Fruit Jam*.
Elderberry Vinegar *see Vinegars*.

F

FIG CHUTNEY

680g (1½lb) green figs, 225g (½lb) onions, 84g (3oz) stoned dates, 56g (2oz) preserved ginger [or 14g (½oz) ground ginger], 570ml (1 pint) vinegar, 225g (½lb) brown sugar, 84g (3oz) stoned raisins, ½tsp. salt, ¼tsp. cayenne.

Slice figs and onions, chop dates and raisins; put vinegar and sugar in pan, bring to boil, simmer 10 min; put all ingredients in basin, pour over hot vinegar; stand overnight, put in pan, bring slowly to boil, and boil gently 2–3 h till dark and thick.

FIG JAM

450g (1lb) green figs, 225g (½lb) cooking apples (when peeled and cored), juice of 3 lemons, grated rind of 1 lemon, 450g (1lb) sugar.

Slice figs and apples; put in pan with lemon rind and juice; simmer very slowly with lid on till tender; add sugar, stirring till dissolved; boil hard for 15 min or to set.

FIG JAM SPICED

*450g (1lb) dried figs, 1.4kg (3lb) cooking apples, juice and rind
3 lemons, 1.1kg (2½lb) sugar, 850ml (1½ pints) water,
1tsp. mixed spice.*

Stalk figs, peel and core apples, rough chop both; put in pan
with water, spices, rind and juice of lemons: simmer till tender;
add sugar, boil 5 min stirring all the time, or till it sets. (If you
do not like fig pips, put through liquidizer and/or sieve before
adding sugar.)

FIG MARMALADE

*450g (1lb) dried figs, 1 lemon, 56g (2oz) preserved ginger
[or 14g (½oz) ground ginger], 225g (½lb) sugar.*

Wash figs, slice thinly, soak in water just to cover overnight; put
in pan, simmer till tender; add sugar, stirring till dissolved; add
grated rind and juice of lemon and ginger (chopped small); simmer till thickened.

FIG PICKLE

*450g (1lb) dried figs, 450g (1lb) Demerara sugar, 285ml
(½ pint) vinegar, 2tsp. ground cloves and cinnamon,
1tsp. ground mace and allspice.*

Wash figs, soak overnight; drain well; put sugar and vinegar in
pan; boil to a syrup, add spices, simmer 1 min; add figs; simmer
gently for 1 h.

FIG PRESERVE (Dried Figs)

*450g (1lb) dried figs, 225g (½lb) rhubarb, juice 1 lemon,
225g (½lb) sugar.*

Wash and chop fruit, put in bowl with lemon juice, cover with sugar; stand overnight; put in pan, bring to boil slowly, stirring, then simmer till thick.

FIG PRESERVE (Fresh Figs)

450g (1lb) ripe figs, 450g (1lb) sugar, juice 1 lemon.

Halve and quarter figs; put in pan with lemon juice and sugar, stirring till dissolved; boil rapidly to set.

FIG PRESERVE (Green Figs)

Follow recipe for fresh figs, using green figs.

FIG AND APPLE JAM

*225g (½lb) dried figs, 850ml (1½ pints) apple juice,
680g (1½lb) sugar, 285ml (½ pint) water.*

Wash and chop figs, boil slowly in water for 1½ h; add apple juice and sugar, stirring till dissolved; boil, stirring frequently to set.

Fig and Apple Preserve *see under Apple.*
Fig and Date Jam *see under Date.*

FIG AND LEMON JAM

*450g (1lb) dried figs, juice of 1 lemon, 680g (1½lb) sugar,
425ml (¾ pint) water.*

Remove stems of figs, wash, chop and soak overnight; drain well; put in pan with water, simmer till tender; add lemon and sugar, stirring till dissolved; cook till thick. (If liked, the grated rind of the lemon may also be added at the same time as the juice.)

FIG AND ORANGE JAM

*450g (1lb) dried figs, 6 oranges, 1.1l (2 pints) water,
1.1kg (2½lb) sugar.*

Wipe oranges and slice very finely, discarding pips; put in bowl with water; stand overnight; put into pan, simmer till tender, add washed and chopped figs and sugar, stirring till dissolved; boil rapidly to set. (It is not essential to stand the oranges overnight but it does improve the flavour.)

Four-Fruit Jam *see Tutti Frutti Jam.*
French Beans, Dried, Pickled or Salted *see under Beans.*

FRUIT SALAD JAM

Follow recipe for Dried Apricot Jam, using dried fruit salad.

FRUIT COCKAIGNE

This is a delicious though expensive surprise for Christmas, and a stone or terracotta jar is required.

Soft fruits (i.e. strawberries, raspberries, loganberries, stoned cherries, redcurrants and blackcurrants, well-ripened gooseberries, sliced apricots, sliced peaches, etc.), 450g (1lb) each, caster sugar, brandy.

As fruits come into season put a layer of fruit, 225g (½lb) sugar and 150ml (¼ pint) brandy (cheapest brandy is adequate), continue with layers till jar is full, and finish by the end of September. Make tight-fitting lid for container and fit firmly. Not to be opened till Christmas Day! This can be used for two purposes – the carefully drained liquid as a liqueur, the drained fruit served with meringue, ice-cream and cream. (This is not a nursery sweet.)

G

Garlic Vinegar *see Vinegars.*
Geranium and Apple Jelly *see under Apple; see also Rose
    Geranium.*

GHERKINS PICKLED

Follow recipe for Pickled Cucumber.

GINGER MARMALADE

*225g (8oz) preserved ginger, 1.4kg (3lb) sharp apples,
570ml (1 pint) water, sugar.*

Wash apples, chop roughly without peeling or coring; simmer in
water till well pulped; strain through jelly bag; finely chop ginger,
put in pan with apple juice and 1kg sugar per kilogram weight
juice and ginger combined (1lb per 1lb); bring slowly to boil, stirring till sugar is dissolved; boil rapidly to set (about 10 min); pot
and cover immediately.

Ginger and Apple Jam *see under Apple*.
Ginger and Cucumber Jam *see under Cucumber*.
Ginger and Lemon Jelly *see under Lemon*.
Ginger and Marrow Jam *see under Marrow*.
Ginger and Melon Jam *see under Melon*.
Ginger and Orange Marmalade *see under Orange*.
Ginger and Pear Jam *see under Pear*.
Ginger and Pear Preserve *see under Pear*.
Ginger and Rhubarb Jam *see under Rhubarb*.
Ginger and Rhubarb Preserve *see under Rhubarb*.
Ginger and Green Tomato Jam *see under Tomato (green)*.

GOOSEBERRY CHEESE

Gooseberries, water, sugar.

Simmer gooseberries in water just to cover; liquidize and/or sieve; return purée to pan with 800g sugar per litre purée (1lb per pint), stirring till dissolved; continue cooking and stirring till thick.

GOOSEBERRY CHUTNEY (1)

450g (1lb) gooseberries, 225g (½lb) raisins, 225g (½lb) onions, 84g (3oz) dark brown sugar, 285ml (½ pint) vinegar, tsp. ground ginger and cayenne, tsp. salt.

Top and tail gooseberries, rough chop onions and raisins; put into pan with all other ingredients; simmer very gently till thick, stirring occasionally. (If you have a very slow oven going, then this can be done in a covered fireproof dish for several hours, but don't forget to stir it from time to time.)

GOOSEBERRY CHUTNEY (2)

450g (1lb) gooseberries, 113g (4oz) cooking apples (when peeled and cored), 225g (½lb) onions (finely chopped), 150ml (¼ pint) vinegar, 170g (6oz) brown sugar, 56g (2oz) sultanas, ½tsp. each ground ginger and mixed spice.

Follow method for Gooseberry Chutney (1).

GOOSEBERRY CONSERVE SPICED

680g (1½lb) gooseberries, 1 orange, 1 lemon, 285ml (½ pint) vinegar, 150ml (¼ pint) water, 113g (4oz) sultanas, 680g (1½lb) brown sugar, 28g (1oz) root ginger, good stick cinnamon, 1 blade mace, 4 cloves.

Tie spices in muslin bag; top and tail gooseberries; put in pan with all ingredients; simmer till fruit is tender and mixture thickens, stirring from time to time. (The longer this conserve matures, the better the flavour.)

GOOSEBERRY CURD

1.4kg (3lb) gooseberries, 680g (1½lb) sugar, 570ml (1 pint) water, 113g (¼lb) butter, 4 eggs.

Top and tail fruit; put in pan with water, simmer till tender; liquidize and/or sieve; put pulp in double saucepan (or bowl over pan of boiling water), add sugar and butter, stirring constantly till all dissolved and well blended; add beaten eggs and continue stirring till mixture thickens; pot and cover when cold.

GOOSEBERRY JAM

1.4kg (3lb) gooseberries (just under-ripe),
1.4kg (3lb) sugar, water.

Top and tail fruit, put into pan, simmer gently 30 min or until fruit is soft enough to mash to a pulp; add sugar, stirring till dissolved; boil rapidly to set. [If a really sharp jam is liked, add the juice of 2 lemons per kilogram gooseberries (1 lemon per lb) at the same time as the sugar.]

GOOSEBERRY JELLY (1)

Gooseberries, sugar, water.

Put gooseberries in pan (no need to top and tail) with 625ml water per kilogram fruit (½ pint per lb); simmer slowly till very soft; strain through jelly bag; put juice in pan with 800g sugar per litre liquid (1lb per pint), stirring till dissolved; boil fast to set.

GOOSEBERRY JELLY (2)

Gooseberries, redcurrant juice, sugar, water.

Cut berries in half, simmer in a little water till tender; crush and strain through jelly bag; put in pan with ¼ litre redcurrant juice and 800g sugar per litre juice (1lb per pint); stir till sugar is dissolved; bring to boil and cook till set; pot and cover when cold.

GOOSEBERRIES SPICED

1.1kg (2½lb) ripe gooseberries, 910g (2lb) brown sugar,
285ml (½ pint) vinegar, 1 tsp each ground
cinnamon and allspice.

Top and tail gooseberries; put in pan with all ingredients; simmer slowly till fruit is tender and mixture thickens, stirring from time to time.

GOOSEBERRY (DESSERT) JELLY (Leveller Jelly)

450g (1lb) very large dessert gooseberries,
150ml (¼ pint) water, sugar.

Follow method for Gooseberry Jelly (1).

Gooseberry and Blackberry Jelly *see under Blackberry.*
Gooseberry and Blackcurrant Jam; Gooseberry and Blackcurrant
  Jelly *follow recipes as for Gooseberry and Redcurrant.*

GOOSEBERRY AND CHERRY JAM

450g (1lb) gooseberries, 570 g (1¼lb) cherries,
910g (2lb) sugar, 150ml (¼ pint) water.

Top and tail gooseberries, stalk and slit cherries; put in pan with water, simmer till tender; remove stones as they rise to the surface; add sugar, stirring till dissolved; boil rapidly to set.

GOOSEBERRY AND LIME JAM

450g (1lb) gooseberries, 4 limes, 710ml (1¼ pints) water, 910g (2lb) sugar.

Top and tail gooseberries, mince limes; put together in pan with water; simmer till soft and crush with wooden spoon; add sugar, stirring till dissolved; then boil 10 min or to set.

GOOSEBERRY AND LOGANBERRY JAM

450g (1lb) gooseberries, 450g (1lb) loganberries, 910g (2lb) sugar, 150ml (¼ pint) water.

Top and tail gooseberries; put in pan with water and simmer 10 min; add loganberries, simmer further 10 min or till fruit is just soft; add sugar, stirring till dissolved; boil fast to set.

GOOSEBERRY AND MINT JELLY

Make basic gooseberry jelly, adding a good bunch of fresh chopped mint whilst cooking before straining; a little freshly chopped mint can be added before potting if liked.

GOOSEBERRY AND ORANGE JAM

680g (1½lb) gooseberries, 2 medium oranges, 680g (1½lb) sugar, 150ml (¼ pint) water.

Top and tail gooseberries; put in pan with water and the grated rind and juice of the oranges; simmer till tender; add sugar, stirring till dissolved, then boil rapidly to set.

GOOSEBERRY AND RASPBERRY JAM

450g (1lb) gooseberries; 450g (1lb) raspberries,
910g (2lb) sugar, 190ml (⅓ pint) water.

Top and tail gooseberries; put in pan with water, simmer till tender, then crush with wooden spoon; add raspberries, cook till soft; add sugar, stirring till dissolved, then boil fast to set.

GOOSEBERRY AND REDCURRANT JAM

910g (2lb) gooseberries, 910g (2lb) sugar,
285ml (½ pint) redcurrant juice.

Top, tail and halve gooseberries; put in pan with redcurrant juice; simmer about 10 min; add sugar, stirring till dissolved, bring *very* slowly to the boil, then boil to set; pot and cover hot.

GOOSEBERRY AND REDCURRANT JELLY

450g (1lb) gooseberries, 450g (1lb) redcurrants,
570ml (1 pint) water.

Simmer gooseberries and redcurrants in water till really soft; strain through jelly bag; put juice in pan with 800g sugar per litre liquid (1lb per pint), stirring till dissolved; boil rapidly to set; pot and cover hot.

GOOSEBERRY AND RHUBARB CONSERVE

450g (1lb) gooseberries, 450g (1lb) rhubarb,
910g (2lb) sugar, juice 1 lemon.

Top and tail gooseberries, trim and cut rhubarb in 12mm (½in) lengths; put together in bowl with sugar and lemon juice; stand several hours or overnight; put in pan, heating very gently and stirring constantly till sugar dissolved; boil fast to gentle set.

GOOSEBERRY AND STRAWBERRY CONSERVE

450g (1lb) gooseberries, 450g (1lb) strawberries, 910g (2lb) sugar, juice 1 lemon.

Top and tail gooseberries, husk strawberries; put together in bowl with sugar and lemon juice; stand several hours or overnight; put in pan, heating very gently and stirring constantly till sugar is dissolved; boil fast to gentle set.

GOOSEBERRY AND STRAWBERRY JAM

450g (1lb) gooseberries, 450g (1lb) strawberries, 910g (2lb) sugar.

Top and tail gooseberries, put in pan with little water; simmer 15 min; husk strawberries; add to pan with sugar, stirring constantly till dissolved; boil, stirring frequently and skimming, till jam sets quickly.

GOOSEBERRY AND STRAWBERRY JELLY (1)

450g (1lb) gooseberries, 450g (1lb) strawberries, 150ml (¼ pint) water, sugar, lemon.

Simmer gooseberries in water till soft, add strawberries; cook till very soft; strain through jelly bag; put liquid in pan allowing juice of 2 lemons and 800g sugar per litre juice (1 lemon, 1lb sugar per pint); stir till sugar dissolved then boil to set.

GOOSEBERRY AND STRAWBERRY JELLY (2)

*450g (1lb) gooseberries, 680g (1½lb) strawberries,
1.3l (2¼ pints) water, sugar.*

Husk strawberries, put in pan with gooseberries and 710ml (1¼ pints) water; simmer till tender; strain through jelly bag; return pulp to pan with further 570ml (1 pint) water, simmer 30 min; strain through jelly bag overnight; put juice in pan with 600g sugar per litre liquid (¾lb per pint), bring to boil stirring till sugar dissolved; boil to set; pot and cover immediately.

Gooseberries *see also Fruit Cockaigne; Mixed Fruit Jam.*

GRAPES (Green or White)

GRAPE CHEESE

450g (1lb) grapes, 450g (1lb) sugar, juice 1 lemon.

Simmer grapes in minimum water till tender; liquidize and/or sieve; put in pan with sugar and lemon juice, stirring till sugar dissolved; then boil rapidly to set.

GRAPE JAM

450g (1lb) grapes, 450g (1lb) sugar.

Wash grapes, simmer gently for 5 min in minimum water; add sugar, stirring till dissolved; then boil fast to set.

PICKLED GRAPES

*450g (1lb) grapes, 150ml (¼ pint) vinegar, 285ml (½ pint)
water, 113g (4oz) sugar, tsp. mixed spice.*

Stalk and wash grapes; pack into jars; boil water, vinegar, sugar
and spices together; strain, allow to cool then pour over grapes
and close down.

GRAPES (Black)

GRAPE JAM

Follow recipe for Green Grape Jam, adding juice of 2 lemons at
the same time as the sugar.

GRAPE JELLY

*450g (1lb) black grapes, 1tbs. lemon juice, 450g (1lb) sugar, ⅓
bottle commercial pectin, 70ml (⅛ pint) water.*

Using ripe grapes, crush in pan with water; cover and simmer for
10 min; strain through jelly bag; put in pan with juice of 2 lemons
and 800g sugar per litre juice (juice 1 lemon, 1lb sugar per pint),
stirring till sugar dissolved; bring to boil; remove from heat, stir
in pectin; bring to fast boil for 1 min; skim, allow to cool; pot and
cover.

GRAPE JELLY SPICED

*450g (1lb) black grapes, 1large cooking apple, 285ml (½ pint)
vinegar, sugar, 150ml (¼ pint) water, small stick cinnamon
and about 15 cloves.*

Tie spices in muslin bag; put all ingredients in pan, simmering
till soft and slightly losing colour; strain through jelly bag; put
juice in pan, with 800g sugar per litre liquid (1lb per pint), stirring till dissolved; boil rapidly to set. (Depending on the type of
grapes used, it may be necessary to add a small quantity of commercial pectin for a set.)

BLACK GRAPE PRESERVE

*1.8kg (4lb) black grapes, 425ml (¾ pint) water,
680g (1¼lb) sugar.*

Wash and stone grapes; put sugar and water in pan, bring to boil
stirring constantly, and boil for 5 min; add grapes, cook till fruit
is clear and syrup thick; pot and cover at once.

GRAPE AND SAVORY JELLY

Follow recipe for Grape Jelly adding 2tbs. dried savory for each
litre juice (1tbs. per pint). (Vary the herbs according to your own
taste using Thyme, Rosemary, etc.; *see Herb Jellies.*)

GRAPEFRUIT CURD

*2 large grapefruit, 113g (4oz) fresh butter,
2 eggs, 225g (½lb) sugar.*

Grate rinds and squeeze juice of fruit; put in double saucepan
with butter and sugar, stirring constantly till completely blended;
beat eggs well, add to mixture and cook, still stirring, till creamy.

GRAPEFRUIT JELLY

910g (2lb) grapefruit, 2 large lemons, sugar, water.

Peel grapefruit and lemons, rough chop peel and fruit (pith, pips, the lot), put in pan with 1.7l (3 pints) water; bring to boil then simmer slowly for about 2 h; strain through jelly bag; put juice in pan with 800g sugar per litre liquid (1lb per pint), stirring till sugar completely dissolved; bring to fast boil for about 5 min or to set; pot and cover at once.

GRAPEFRUIT MARMALADE

*2 grapefruit, 2 lemons, 1.7l (3 pints) water,
2.3kg (5lb) sugar.*

Fine slice or chop fruit as preferred; put pips in muslin bag; put all in bowl with water; cover and stand overnight; put in pan, simmer till tender; add sugar, stirring till dissolved; then boil fairly fast to set.

Grapefruit and Orange Marmalade *see under Orange.*
Grapefruit, Orange and Lemon Marmalade *see Three-Fruit Marmalade.*

GRAPEFRUIT AND TANGERINE JELLY

*2 grapefruit, 3 tangerines, 2 lemons,
3.1l (5½ pints) water, sugar.*

Wash fruit, coarse chop; put in pan with water and boil 2 h; strain through jelly bag overnight; return pulp to pan, add water just to cover; boil 1 h; strain again; put juice in pan with 800g sugar per litre liquid (1lb per pint), stirring till dissolved; boil 10 min or to set; pot and cover immediately.

Grapefruit and Rhubarb Jam *see under Rhubarb.*

GREENGAGE JAM

910g (2lb) greengages (stalked and stoned),
680g (1½lb) sugar, water.

Put fruit in pan with small quantity of water; bring to boil and simmer gently 15 min; add sugar, stirring till dissolved; bring to boil and boil gently to set; pot and cover at once.

GREENGAGE JELLY

910g (2lb) greengages, 285ml (½ pint) water, sugar.

Halve greengages, simmer in water (a little more may be needed if fruit is very firm) till soft; strain through jelly bag; put juice in pan with 800g sugar per litre liquid (1lb per pint); stir till sugar dissolved; then boil steadily to set; pot and cover at once.

GREENGAGE AND APPLE JAM

910g (2lb) stoned greengages, 450g (1lb) cooking apples (when peeled and cored), 150ml (¼ pint) water, 1.4kg (3lb) sugar.

Put fruit in pan with water, simmer till soft; add sugar, stirring till dissolved; boil steadily to set; pot and cover at once. (If greengages are very ripe, allow apple to cook for short time first.)

GREENGAGE AND RED PLUM JAM

*450g (1lb) stoned greengages, 450g (1lb) stoned red plums,
910g (2lb) sugar, 150ml (¼ pint) water.*

Proceed as for Greengage Jam.

GUAVA JAM

450g (1lb) guava pulp, 450g (1lb) sugar, juice 1 lemon.

Simmer pulp in very little water till soft; add lemon juice and
sugar, stirring till dissolved; boil fast to set.

GUAVA JELLY

Guavas, sugar, lime juice.

Wash and quarter guavas, just cover with water; bring to boil,
simmer 30 min; strain through jelly bag; put in pan with 800g
sugar and 2tsp. lime juice per litre liquid (1tsp. per pint); stir till
sugar dissolved; boil rapidly to set; pot and cover at once.

H

HAW JELLY

1.4kg (3lb) haws, 1.7l (3 pints) water, sugar, lemons.

Well wash haws, put in pan with water; simmer 1 h; strain through jelly bag; put juice in pan with juice of 2 lemons and 800g sugar per litre liquid (1lb per pint); stir till sugar dissolved; boil rapidly to set; pot and cover at once.

HAW SAUCE

680g (1½lb) haws, 113g (4oz) sugar, 28g (1oz) salt, 425ml (¾ pint) vinegar, ½tsp. white pepper.

Wash fruit well, put in pan with vinegar; simmer gently 30 min; liquidize and/or sieve; return to pan with sugar, salt and pepper, bring to boil; boil rapidly for 10 min; bottle and seal at once; this is a very good 'keeper'.

HEDGEROW JAM

225g (½lb) each rosehips, hawthorn hips, rowanberries and sloes, 450g (1lb) each elderberries, blackberries and crabapples, 113g (4oz) hazelnuts, 2.3kg (5lb) sugar, 2.3l (4 pints) water.

Wash fruit, stalk, top and tail as necessary; peel and core crabapples, shell hazelnuts; put all in pan with 2.3l (4 pints) water, simmer till soft; add sugar, stirring till dissolved; boil rapidly to set.

HERBS DRIED

Pick herbs in good condition; tie in bunches and hang up with plenty of air around for about 48 h; put in paper bag (not grease-proof) in dark, dry place; when thoroughly dried, remove from stalks, crumble and store in airtight jars.

HERB JELLIES

Use any good basic, 'soft flavoured' jelly, i.e. apples, gooseberry, white grape, etc., and add a bunch of fresh herbs during the cooking time and remove at setting point. If liked, a small quantity of fresh chopped herb can be added to each jar when potting. Dried herbs can be used, but tie in fine muslin bag during cooking.

HORSERADISH DRIED

Wash, scrape and finely grate the horseradish; spread on flat tin and dry in very cool oven; when absolutely dried, store in airtight containers.

Horseradish and Beetroot Relish *see under Beetroot Relish*.
Horseradish and Red Tomato Relish *see under Tomato (red)*.

HUCKLEBERRY JAM

Follow recipe for Bilberry Jam.

I

INDIAN CHUTNEY (1)

*680g (1½lb) sharp apples (when peeled and cored), 1 large
onion, 570ml (1 pint) vinegar, 450g (1lb) Barbados sugar,
225g (½lb) stoned raisins, 113g (4oz) crystallized ginger, ½tsp.
cayenne pepper, 1tsp. salt, 2tsp. dry mustard.*

Quarter apples (having peeled, cored and weighed), finely chop
onion; boil together in vinegar to a pulp; add sugar, chopped
raisins, finely cut ginger and spices; stir well together; boil for 30
min, stirring frequently; pot and cover. (Do give this good time to
mature before use.)

INDIAN CHUTNEY (2)

*450g (1lb) sour apples (peeled, cored and sliced), 225g (½lb)
onions, 450g (1lb) dark brown sugar, 225g (½lb) stoned
raisins, 113g (4oz) salt, 113g (4oz) ground ginger, 56g (2oz)
dry mustard, 14g (½oz) cayenne, 2 cloves garlic,
1.1l (2 pints) vinegar.*

Put sliced apples, coarsely chopped onions in pan with garlic,
salt, sugar and vinegar; simmer till tender; put through coarse
mincer, and remaining ingredients, mix well together; stand in
warm place till next day; pot and cover closely. (This should keep
for up to 2 years.)

INDIAN RELISH

1.8kg (4lb) green tomatoes, 1 green pepper, 1 red pepper,
1 head drumhead cabbage, 3 large onions, 113g (4oz) salt,
piece horseradish root, 680g (1½lb) brown sugar,
1tsp. each cinnamon, nutmeg, allspice, celery seed
and mustard seed, vinegar.

Halve peppers and remove seeds; chop or coarse mince all vegetables; put in basin, grate on horseradish root, sprinkle with salt; stand overnight; drain well; put in pan, cover with cold vinegar, bring to boil and drain; cover with fresh vinegar, add spices and sugar, heat to boiling, cook 5 min, pot and seal. (This keeps well, and also makes a fair quantity so be sure you like a really hot taste before embarking on it.)

J

JAPONICA JAM

910g (2lb) japonicas, 4 lemons, 1.1l (2 pints) water, sugar,
ground ginger to taste.

Cut japonicas in half, simmer in water till tender; liquidize and
/ or coarse sieve; return to pan with 1kg sugar per kilogram pulp
(1lb per lb), with juice of lemons and ginger to flavour, stirring till
sugar is dissolved; boil rapidly to set.

JAPONICA JELLY

910g (2lb) japonicas, 1.1 l (2 pints) water, sugar.

Quarter fruit, put in pan with water; simmer till tender; strain
through jelly bag; put juice in pan with 800g sugar to each litre
liquid (1lb per pint), stirring till sugar dissolved; boil to set; pot
and cover immediately.

JERUSALEM ARTICHOKES PICKLED

Artichokes, salt, water, spiced vinegar.

Wash and scrape artichokes; cook in salt and water [45g salt per
litre water (1oz per pint)] until just tender; drain well; when cold,
pack into jars; cover with cold spiced vinegar and seal down.

K

KUMQUAT PRESERVE

1.4kg (3lb) kumquats, water, sugar, honey.

Cut fruit in slices (remove pips); put in pan with water to just cover; bring to boil, simmer 15 min; strain; put liquid in pan and for each litre juice add 800g sugar and 300g honey (1lb sugar, 6oz honey per pint); simmer for 5 min, add drained fruit, and cook till transparent (approx. 45 min); remove fruit carefully to jars, boil syrup till thick, cover fruit and seal down.

L

Lemon Cheese *see Lemon Curd.*

LEMON CHUTNEY

2 large lemons, 113g (¼lb) onions, 56g (2oz) sultanas, 14g
(½oz) salt, mustard seed and ground ginger, pinch cayenne
pepper, 225g (½lb) sugar, 210 ml (⅜ pint) vinegar.

Wash lemons, slice finely, remove pips; finely chop onions; put
both in a bowl, sprinkle with salt, stand overnight; put in pan,
with very little water, simmer till tender; add all other ingredients, bring to boil and simmer till thick (about 1 h). (For a lighter
coloured chutney, use white vinegar.)

LEMON CURD

1 lemon, 56g (2oz) butter, 113g (4oz) sugar, 3 eggs.

Put butter, sugar, grated rind and strained juice of lemon in double
saucepan; cook very slowly, stirring till melted and well blended;
remove from heat; beat eggs, add slowly to mixture, stirring all
the time; return to heat and keep stirring till thickened.

LEMON CURD (MOCK)

*1 lemon, 150ml (¼ pint) water, 113g (¼lb) sugar, 1 egg,
1tsp. cornflour, knob of butter or margarine.*

Put water, sugar, grated rind of lemon and knob of butter in double saucepan; when butter has melted, add cornflour mixed with
juice of lemon; simmer gently, stirring till thickening; remove
from heat; beat egg well, add to mixture, return to heat and simmer a few more minutes, stirring all the time.

LEMON JELLY

Lemons, sugar, water.

Weigh lemons, wash, cut in quarters, remove pips; put in large
bowl, just covering with water, stand overnight; put in pan, boil
for 2 h; strain through jelly bag; put juice in pan with 800g sugar
per litre liquid (1lb per pint), stirring till sugar dissolved; boil to
set. (This jelly is a very good basis for herb and spiced jellies.)

LEMON MARMALADE

12 lemons, sugar, water.

Wash lemons, put in pan with water to cover; boil till soft;
remove from pan, cut in half, scoop out pulp; discarding pith and
pips; slice peel thinly; put in pan with pulp and weigh (to do this
weigh pan first, then with fruit in, then subtract to get weight of
fruit); add equal quantity of sugar and 630ml of water in which
lemons were boiled for each kilogram fruit (½ pint per pound);
stir till sugar dissolved, then boil to set; pot and cover at once.

LEMON PICKLE

450g (1lb) lemons, 3 tbs. salt, 1tsp. turmeric, 1½tsp. chilli powder, 2tsp. allspice (or if liked hot, 1tsp. all-spice, 1tsp. curry powder); 150–285ml (¼–½ pint) white vinegar.

Cut fruit into chunks, remove pips; do this on a plate to catch as much juice as possible; put into bowl with all other ingredients and mix thoroughly; transfer to screw-top jar and keep in sun or warm place for 1 week, shaking every day; when skins are tender, the pickle is ready. [If a sweet pickle is preferred, add 84g (3oz) Demerara sugar.]

LEMONS PICKLED

Lemons, salt, turmeric, garlic, small onions, cloves, root ginger, peppercorns, mustard seed, white wine vinegar.

Wipe lemons, make four slits from end to end without cutting through; stuff slits with salt and slither of garlic, put in bowl; cover and stand in warm place for 10 days, turning daily and basting with liquid; remove lemons, rub each with turmeric; put in large jar, adding 1 small lemon spiked with cloves for each lemon; cover with the juices; boil together 570ml (1 pint) white wine vinegar with 56g (2oz) bruised root ginger, 14g (½oz) peppercorns and 56g (2oz) mustard seed, all tied in muslin bag (or proportions of these quantities to completely cover lemons); pour hot over lemons, cover jar with plate; next day add six small chillies and fasten jar down.

LEMON AND APPLE CURD

*3 lemons, 2 large cooking apples, 225g (8oz) sugar,
113g (4oz) butter, 2 eggs.*

Bake apples in oven till they collapse; remove pulp, then proceed
as for Lemon Curd. (If you want this curd to keep well double
the amount of sugar.)

Lemon and Apple Jam; Lemon and Apple Jelly *see under Apple.*

LEMON AND APPLE MARMALADE

*6 lemons, 450g (1lb) cooking apples, 6 cloves,
1 medium stick cinnamon, sugar.*

Peel lemons very thinly then slice, removing pith and pips; put
in bowl, with water just to cover; stand overnight; peel, core and
slice apples, put in pan with very little water, simmer till tender;
add lemon peel, fruit and juice to apple with cloves and cinnamon
in muslin bag; boil for 1 h; stand for 24 h in clean bowl; return to
pan with 1kg sugar per kilogram fruit mixture (1lb sugar per lb
fruit), stirring till dissolved, then boil to set.

Lemon and Banana Jam *see under Banana.*
Lemon and Date Chutney *see under Date.*
Lemon and Fig Jam *see under Fig.*

LEMON AND GINGER JELLY

Follow recipe for Lemon Jelly, adding 113g (4oz) bruised ginger
(in muslin bag) whilst the lemons soak overnight.

Lemon, Grapefruit and Orange Marmalade *see under Three-Fruit Marmalade.*

Lemon and Marrow Curd; Lemon and Marrow Jam *see under Marrow.*

Lemon and Medlar Jelly *see under Medlar.*

Lemon and Melon Jam *see under Melon.*

Lemon and Orange Chutney; Lemon and Orange Curd *see under Orange.*

LEMON AND ORANGE JELLY

3 large lemons, 1 Seville orange, sugar.

Thinly slice peel from fruit and put in muslin bag; rough chop fruit, put in pan with 2 pints (1.2l) water (and the muslin bag), simmer for 1½ h; remove and retain muslin bag; strain fruit through jelly bag; put juice in pan with 800g sugar per litre liquid (1lb per pint); stirring till dissolved, then add muslin bag again; bring to rapid boil for about 5 min, or to set; remove muslin bag; cool for about 20 min then pot and cover immediately.

Lemon and Seville Orange Marmalade *see under Orange.*

LEMON AND SWEET ORANGE MARMALADE

*3 lemons, 2 sweet oranges, 1.4l (2½ pints) water,
910g (2lb) sugar.*

Follow recipe for Lemon Marmalade.

Lemon and Pear Jam *see under Pear.*

LEMON AND PINEAPPLE PRESERVE

2 lemons, 1 small pineapple, 1.4l (2½ pints) water, sugar.

Wipe lemons, slice finely, removing pips to muslin bag, and put all in bowl with water to soak overnight; put in pan, simmer till tender, return to bowl, removing pip bag; stand overnight; chop pineapple on dish to keep maximum juice, put in pan with lemon and juice, weight, add 800g sugar per litre pulp (1lb per pint), stirring till dissolved; boil rapidly to set.

Lemon and Pumpkin Jam *see under Pumpkin*.
Lemon and Rhubarb Marmalade *see under Rhubarb*.

LEMON AND TANGERINE MARMALADE

2 lemons, 3 tangerines, 710ml (1¼ pints) water,
800g (1¾lb) sugar.

Wash fruit, remove skins and shred finely; remove pith and pips to muslin bag; put all in pan with water; simmer till tender and mixture thick, stirring from time to time; remove muslin bag, pressing to release all possible moisture; add sugar, stirring till dissolved, bring to fast boil for 10 min or to set.

Lemon and Tomato Conserve *see under Tomato*.

LEMON AND VERBENA JELLY

Add 2 verbena leaves to each 285ml (½ pint) lemon juice, and remove before potting.

Leveller Jelly *see under Gooseberry (dessert)*.

LIME MARMALADE

450g (1lb) limes, 1.4l (2½ pints) water, 1.1kg (2½lb) sugar.

Finely cut limes, removing pips to muslin bag; soak all overnight in water to cover; put in pan, simmer till peel is soft (approx. 1½ h); remove pips, add sugar, stirring till dissolved, bring to fast boil for 20 min or to set.

LIME PICKLE

Follow recipe as for Lemon Pickle.

LIMES PICKLED

Follow recipe as for Lemons Pickled.

Lime and Gooseberry Jam *see under Gooseberry.*
Lime and Tangerine Marmalade *see under Tangerine.*

LOGANBERRY CHEESE

450g (1lb) loganberries, 450g (1lb) sugar, water.

Simmer loganberries in water just to cover till really soft; liquidize and/or sieve; return to pan, add sugar, stirring till dissolved; cook till thick.

LOGANBERRY JAM

450g (1lb) loganberries, 450g (1lb) sugar, water.

Simmer fruit in 570ml (1 pint) water till tender; add sugar, stirring till dissolved, boil fast to set.

LOGANBERRY JELLY

910g (2lb) loganberries, 150ml (¼ pint) water, sugar.

Choose fruit when just ripe, put in pan with water; simmer very slowly for about 1 h; strain through jelly bag; return to pan with 800g sugar for each litre juice (1lb per pint), stirring till dissolved; boil fast to set; pot and cover at once.

Loganberry and Blackcurrant Jam; Loganberry and Blackcurrant Jelly *follow recipe as for Loganberry and Redcurrant.*

LOGANBERRY AND CHERRY JAM

450g (1lb) loganberries, 450g (1lb) cooking cherries, 910g (2lb) sugar, juice of 1 lemon, water.

Slit cherries, put in pan with very little water; simmer 10 min; add loganberries; simmer till soft; add sugar, stirring till dissolved; boil rapidly to set, removing cherry stones as they rise to the surface.

Loganberry and Gooseberry Jam *see under Gooseberry.*

LOGANBERRY AND RASPBERRY JAM

450g (1lb) loganberries, 450g (1lb) raspberries, 910g (2lb) sugar.

Simmer loganberries in very little water till tender; add raspberries, simmer further 5 min; add sugar, stirring till dissolved; boil fast to set.

LOGANBERRY AND REDCURRANT JAM

450g (1lb) loganberries, 450g (1lb) redcurrants,
910g (2lb) sugar, 150ml (¼ pint) water.

Put fruit in pan, simmer till soft; add sugar, stirring till dissolved; boil fast to set.

LOGANBERRY AND REDCURRANT JELLY

450g (1lb) loganberries, 450g (1lb) redcurrants,
570ml (1 pint) water, sugar.

Put fruit in pan with water and simmer till very soft; strain through jelly bag; put juice in pan with 800g sugar per litre liquid (1lb per pint), stirring well till dissolved; boil rapidly to set; pot and cover at once.

LOGANBERRY AND RHUBARB JAM

450g (1lb) loganberries, 450g (1lb) rhubarb,
910g (2lb) sugar, 150ml (¼ pint) water.

Cut and trim rhubarb, put in pan with water and simmer gently till tender; add loganberries; simmer till soft; add sugar, stirring till dissolved; boil fast to set.

LOGANBERRY AND STRAWBERRY JAM

450g (1lb) loganberries, 450g (1lb) strawberries,
910g (2lb) sugar, water.

Put fruit in pan with very little water; simmer gently for 30 min; add sugar, stirring till dissolved; boil fast to set.

Loganberries *see also Fruit Cockaigne, Mixed Fruit Jam.*

LYCHEE JAM

450g (1lb) shelled fresh lychees, 400g (14oz) sugar,
juice 1 lemon.

Simmer all together, stirring till sugar dissolved; remove stones, boil gently to set.

LYCHEE PRESERVE

Tinned lychees, sugar, lemon juice.

Drain fruit and weigh; allow ½kg sugar per kilogram fruit (½lb sugar per lb fruit); put juice from tin in pan, add sugar, stirring till dissolved, then boil to thick syrup, add lemon juice to taste; add fruit; simmer 10 min.

M

MANGO CHUTNEY (1)

8 green mangoes, 570ml (1 pint) vinegar, 225g (½lb) sugar,
225g (½lb) stoned tamarinds, 84g (3oz) stoned raisins,
84g (3oz) salt, ½tsp. nutmeg and cinnamon,
84g (3oz) bruised ginger (in muslin bag).

Peel and slice mangoes very finely, put in bowl, sprinkle with salt;
stand 48 h; put 285ml (½ pint) vinegar in pan with sugar and boil
to a syrup, add remaining vinegar and mangoes, simmer for 10
min; add all remaining ingredients, simmer very slowly for 30–40
min, till quite syrupy. [If you can obtain green ginger, use 84g
(3oz) sliced instead of the root ginger in muslin bag.]

MANGO CHUTNEY (2)

450g (1lb) mangoes, 225g (½lb) cooking apples (when peeled
and cored), 170g (6oz) onions, 280g (10oz) brown sugar, 1tsp.
ground ginger, 1tsp. pickling spice (in muslin bag),
½tsp. salt, 570ml (1 pint) vinegar.

Slice mangoes very finely, rough chop apples, put in bowl, sprinkle
with salt; stand overnight; put in pan with fine chopped onions
and all other ingredients (except sugar); simmer gently till fruit
and onions are soft; remove spice bag, add sugar, stirring till dissolved, then boil till thick.

MANGOLD CHUTNEY

910g (2lb) mangolds, 225g (½lb) shallots, 170g (6oz) sugar,
850ml (1½ pints) spiced vinegar (see Vinegars),
2tsp. turmeric.

Peel and cut mangolds into small cubes, rough chop shallots; put both in bowl, sprinkle with salt; stand overnight; strain; put in pan with sugar and vinegar; boil about 1 h; add turmeric, boil further 5 min.

MARJORAM JELLY

Follow recipe for Lemon Jelly, adding 3½tbs. fresh chopped marjoram per litre liquid (2tbs. per pint). If you prefer a clear jelly, add marjoram to lemons before straining through jelly bag.

Marmalade *see under Lemon, Orange, Grapefruit, etc.*

MARROW CHUTNEY (1)

1.8kg (4lb) marrow, 3 large onions, 225g (½lb) sugar, 1.7l
(3 pints) vinegar, 6 chillies, 8 cloves, 14g (½oz) each ground
ginger, dry mustard and turmeric, salt.

Peel and seed marrow, cut in cubes, sprinkle with salt; stand overnight; drain well, put in pan with all other ingredients, bring to boil, stirring from time to time, simmer till tender and thickened.

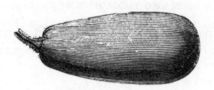

MARROW CHUTNEY (2)

*1.4kg (3lb) marrow, 225g (½lb) onions, 225g (½lb) sultanas,
225g (½lb) apples (peeled and cored), 113g (4oz) sugar,
12 peppercorns, 7g (¼oz) bruised ginger,
850ml (1½ pints) vinegar, salt.*

Proceed as above, but put ginger and peppercorns into muslin bag and remove before potting.

MARROW CREAM OR CURD

*910g (2lb) marrow (when peeled and cored), 450g (1lb) sugar,
2 lemons, 113g (4oz) butter.*

Peel and seed marrow, boil in water till soft, strain well then liquidize or mash to smooth pulp; put into double saucepan with sugar, butter and the juice and grated rind of the lemons, and cook, stirring frequently, till creamy and thick.

Marrow Pickle *see Marrow Chutney.*

MARROW AND APRICOT JAM

*910g (2lb) prepared marrow, 225g (½lb) dried apricots, 1.4kg
(3lb) sugar, 850ml (1½ pints) water, 2 lemons.*

Soak apricots overnight; put in pan and simmer till tender; prepare marrow, and in another pan simmer with very small quantity of water until tender, then mash to pulp; combine marrow and apricots, add grated rind and juice of lemons and sugar; bring to boil, stirring till sugar dissolved; boil fast for about 20 min or to firm consistency.

MARROW AND BLACKBERRY CHUTNEY

910g (2lb) prepared marrow, 450g (1lb) blackberries, 450g (1lb) apples (when peeled and cored), 225g (½lb) onions, 225g (½lb) sultanas, 225g (½lb) sugar, 285ml (½ pint) vinegar, 1tsp. each ground ginger, mixed spice, dry mustard and cayenne.

Prepare fruit and vegetables and put in pan with all ingredients; bring slowly to the boil and simmer gently till cooked and slightly thick, stirring from time to time.

Marrow and Blackberry Jam *see under Blackberry*.
Marrow and Damson Jam *see under Damson*.

MARROW AND GINGER JAM

910g (2lb) prepared marrow, 910g (2lb) sugar, 1 lemon, 113g (4oz) crystallized ginger (or 1tsp. ground ginger).

Prepare marrow, put in bowl and sprinkle with salt; stand all day; rinse and drain well, return to bowl, cover with sugar; stand overnight; put in pan with juice and rind of lemon and the ginger chopped finely; boil slowly till marrow is transparent; pot and cover when cold. (There are many variations of this preserve, but despite the standing time, which in any case can be useful, doing a bit at a time, I like this one found in a 'Granny's' handwritten book.)

MARROW LEMON CURD

Marrow, sugar, butter, eggs, lemons.

Peel, seed and rough cut marrow; simmer very slowly without water till soft, then liquidize or sieve; for each ½kg/½lb pulp allow ½kg/½lb sugar, 125g/2½oz butter, 2 eggs, the rind of 3 and the juice of 2 lemons, and proceed as for lemon curd. (This is an excellent economical recipe when lemons are expensive.)

MARROW AND LEMON JAM

Marrow, sugar, lemons.

Peel marrow, remove seeds, cut in cubes and weigh; put in bowl with equal weight of sugar and the grated rind and juice of 4 lemons for each kilogram marrow (2 lemons per lb); stand overnight; put in pan, simmer gently, stirring till sugar is dissolved, until marrow is transparent and juice syrupy.

MARROW AND ORANGE CURD

Follow recipe for Marrow Lemon Curd, substituting oranges for lemons.

MARROW AND ORANGE JAM

Follow recipe for Marrow and Lemon Jam using rind and juice of 4 oranges and 2 lemons per kilogram marrow (2 oranges and 1 lemon per lb).

MARROW AND PINEAPPLE JAM

Marrow, sugar, pineapple chunks.

Peel and seed marrow, cut in chunks and stand in bowl with 600g sugar per kilogram marrow; stand overnight; put in pan with drained pineapple chunks (1 large tin/1 small tin per kilogram/ per lb marrow), simmer all together, stirring till sugar is dissolved, until pineapple is soft and syrup sets. (If you want to be wildly extravagant, ½ kg fresh pineapple chunks per kilogram marrow (½lb per lb) is most acceptable!)

MARROW AND PLUM JAM

910g (2lb) prepared marrow, 910g (2lb) plums,
1.8kg (4lb) sugar.

Peel, seed and dice marrow; put in bowl with 910g (2lb) sugar and stand overnight; put in pan, simmer till nearly tender; add stoned plums (crack some stones for kernels) and cook till soft; add remaining sugar and kernels, stir till sugar dissolved, bring to boil, and boil slowly to set.

Marrow and Quince Jam *see under Quince.*
Marrow and Tomato Chutney *see under Tomato (red).*

MEDLAR CHEESE

910g (2lb) medlars, 2 lemons, 285ml (½ pint) water, 1tsp.
mixed spice, sugar.

Wash medlars and quarter; peel lemons, squeeze juice, put peel and pips in muslin bag; put in pan with fruit, water and lemon juice; simmer till tender; remove muslin bag; liquidize and/or sieve fruit; return to pan with ¾kg sugar and 2tsp. spice per kilogram pulp (¾lb sugar, 1 tsp. spice, per lb), stirring till sugar is dissolved; bring to boil; boil fast to thickening.

MEDLAR JAM

910g (2lb) medlars, 2 lemons, 850ml (1½ pints) water, sugar.

Follow recipe for Medlar Cheese; this makes a less stiff preserve.

MEDLAR JELLY

450g (1lb) medlars, 285ml (½ pint) water, sugar.

Quarter fruit, put in pan with water; simmer till tender; strain through jelly bag; put juice in pan with 600g sugar per litre liquid (¾lb per pint); boil to set; pot and cover at once.

MEDLAR AND LEMON JELLY

Follow recipe for Medlar Jelly, adding grated rind and juice of 4 lemons per kilogram medlars (2 lemons per lb) whilst cooking before straining.

MELON JAM

910g (2lb) melon (peeled and seeded), 680g (1½lb) sugar.

Cut melon into cubes, put in bowl with layers of sugar; stand in cool place 3 h; put in pan, bring to boil, stirring till sugar dissolved; boil fast to set.

MELON MARMALADE

Melon, sugar.

Peel and seed melon, liquidize and/or sieve flesh; put in pan with ¼kg sugar per kilogram pulp (¼lb per lb); boil to set.

MELON PICKLE

Small green melons, salt, vinegar, pickling spice.

Cut melon in convenient sizes, discarding pips, but not peeling; put in bowl, sprinkle with salt; stand overnight; drain well, leave in sieve to dry, or wipe each piece with a clean cloth; put in bowl with cold boiled vinegar; stand overnight; drain off vinegar into pan and bring to boil with 50g pickling spice (in muslin bag) per litre vinegar (1oz per pint); put melon pieces in jar, cover with hot spiced vinegar; seal down.

MELON PRESERVE

Melons (slightly under-ripe), water, sugar, lemon, root ginger.

Slice melon thinly, leaving on peel but removing seeds; bring pan of water to boil, throw in melon, leave for 3 min; drain well; weigh; return to pan with 1kg (1lb) sugar, 1.25l (1 pint) water, grated rind of 2 lemons (1 lemon) and a piece (small slice) of root ginger (in muslin bag) for each kilogram (lb) fruit; bring to boil, stirring very gently; simmer 5 min; carefully remove fruit to large jar; skim syrup if necessary and pour over fruit; stand for 3 days; drain syrup, boil up again, pour hot over melon and cover closely.

MELON AND GINGER JAM

Proceed as for Melon Jam, add 56g (2oz) chopped crystallized ginger whilst standing, and the juice of 2 lemons during cooking.

MELON AND LEMON JAM

Proceed as for Melon Jam, adding the grated rind and juice of 4 lemons per kilogram fruit whilst standing (2 lemons per lb).

MELON AND PINEAPPLE PRESERVE

450g (1lb) melon (when peeled and seeded), 450g (1lb) pineapple when peeled, 910g (2lb) sugar, juice 2 lemons.

Cut fruit into cubes on a plate, to catch as much juice as possible, put in pan with lemon juice and simmer very slowly till just tender; add sugar, stirring till dissolved; then boil rapidly to set.

MINCEMEAT

This is a preserve that has so many variations it is difficult to know where to start. Originally, mincemeat did have meat in it, so for recipe (1) I will give this, as it is the only one where any cooking is required. In all other cases the ingredients are finely chopped, mixed well together, then the rum and brandy added and mixed in well, and stood for at least two months to mature.

(1) *450g (1lb) lean beef, 910g (2lb) beef suet, 910g (2lb) moist sugar, 1.4kg (3lb) currants, 450g (1lb) mixed candied peel, 340g (¾lb) mixed peel, grated rind of 6 lemons, juice of 2 lemons, 28g (1oz) mixed spice.*

Stew beef till tender, chop finely (or coarse mince) and when cold mix with all other ingredients; pot and cover closely. Finely chopped tongue may be used instead of beef and, before using, a small quantity of fresh chopped apple mixed well in.

(2) *450g (1lb) currants, 450g (1lb) sultanas, 450g (1lb) coarse chopped raisins, 680g (1½lb) beef suet, 450g (1lb) brown sugar, 28g (1oz) mixed spice, 450g (1lb) peeled, cored and chopped apples, grated rind and juice of 2 lemons and 3 oranges, rum or brandy, or a mixture of both, to just moisten.*

(3) *910g (2lb) apples, peeled, cored and chopped, 450g (1lb) kidney suet, 910g (2lb) dark brown sugar, 450g (1lb) each chopped raisins, sultanas and currants, 225g (½lb) candied peel finely chopped, 113g (¼lb) blanched almonds, 28g (1oz) mixed spice, brandy to moisten.*

(4) *1.4kg (3lb) beef suet, 1.4kg (3lb) apples, peeled, cored and chopped, 1.8kg (4lb) currants, 450g (1lb) chopped raisins, 225g (½lb) dark brown sugar, 14g (½oz) each ground clove and cinnamon, 570ml (1 pint) brandy.*

(5) *1.8kg (4lb) beef suet, 2.3kg (5lb) apples, peeled, cored and chopped, 1.8kg (4lb) mixed lemon, orange and citron peel finely chopped, 910g (2lb) dark brown sugar, 2tsp. nutmeg; other spices to personal taste, 285ml (½ pint) brandy.*

(6) *For immediate use. 113g (¼lb) each sultanas, currants and chopped raisins, 1tbs. fine chopped dessert apple, 56g (2oz) candied peel, 56g (2oz) chopped glacé cherries, 1 banana, 84g (3oz) brown sugar, grated rind and juice 1 small lemon, 2tbs. sherry.*

(This does not keep.)

As you will see the ingredients are more or less the same, the difference lies mainly in the variations of the quantities used. Just one note – if time is not all that important, do use fresh suet from your butcher and grate or mince it yourself.

MINT CHUTNEY (1)

*113g (¼lb) fresh mint, 1 small onion, lemon juice,
salt, black and red pepper.*

Chop mint and onion and pound well together; season with salt and pepper and moisten with lemon juice to a thick paste.

MINT CHUTNEY (2)

*225g (½lb) fresh mint, 450g (1lb) onions, 225g (½lb) green
tomatoes, 450g (1lb) cooking apples, 340g (¾lb) sultanas,
2tsp. each salt and dry mustard, 570ml (1 pint) vinegar,
450g (1lb) dark brown sugar.*

Wash mint and drain well; finely chop onions and mint, halve and quarter tomatoes; peel, core and rough chop apples (if preferred all these ingredients may be put through a coarse mincer together); put in pan with 425ml (¾ pint) vinegar and all other ingredients except sugar, and simmer gently till tender; make a syrup of remaining vinegar and sugar, add to mint mixture, bring to boil; simmer about 20 min or till thickened.

MINT JELLY (1)

*113g (¼lb) mint, 1tbs. sugar, 1tbs. water, basic jelly recipe
(apple, lemon, whitecurrant, etc., according to preference).*

Wash and finely chop mint, put in bowl with sugar and water;
stand overnight; add 2tbs. to each litre of basic jelly (1tbs. per
pint) when boiling to set; pot and cover immediately.

MINT JELLY (2)

*225g (8oz) mint leaves, 225g (½lb) lump sugar, 285ml
(½ pint) white vinegar, 285ml (½ pint) water, gelatine
as per directions.*

Wash and finely chop mint; dissolve sugar in vinegar and
water, add mint and moistened gelatine; strain and pot; cover
immediately.

If you prefer a clear jelly, strain before potting and if a darker
colour is liked, add a few drops of green colouring matter at the
last minute.

MINT MARMALADE

Follow recipe for Lemon Marmalade, adding 2tbs. fresh chopped
mint for each kilogram preserve (1tbs. per pound).

Mint Vinegar *see Vinegars.*
Mint and Apple Chutney *see under Apple.*
Mint and Gooseberry Chutney *see under Gooseberry.*

MINT AND HONEY JELLY

2tbs. fresh chopped mint leaves, 285ml (½ pint) water, 450g (1lb) clear honey, ½ bottle pectin, green colouring.

Boil water, pour over finely chopped mint leaves; stand for 15–30 min; strain liquid into pan with honey, bring to boil, add colouring; bring to fast boil, remove from heat and add pectin; boil further 1 min skimming if necessary; pot and cover immediately.

Mint and Pineapple Jelly *see under Pineapple.*

MINT AND REDCURRANT JELLY

Follow basic recipe for Redcurrant Jelly, adding good bunch of fresh mint whilst simmering before straining and, if liked, a few pieces of fresh chopped mint before potting.

MIXED FRUIT JAM

910g (2lb) mixed soft fruits, 1.1kg (2½lb) sugar, water.

Put prepared soft fruits in pan with a little water (the amount will depend on the ripeness of the fruit); simmer till tender; add sugar, stirring till dissolved; boil to set; pot and cover at once.

(This is a very useful way of using up odd small quantities of strawberries, raspberries, loganberries, gooseberries, etc.)

MIXED PICKLED FRUITS

910g (2lb) mixed fruits (when prepared, i.e. crabapples,
damsons, peaches, plums, apricots, etc.), 450g (1lb) sugar,
285ml (½ pint) white vinegar, 1tsp. pickling spice
in muslin bag.

Simmer spices in vinegar for 10 min and remove muslin bag; add
sugar, stirring till dissolved, then add the prepared fruits; simmer
till tender; remove fruits carefully to jar(s), boil liquid for a few
minutes till thickened; pour over fruits and close down at once.

MIXED PICKLES

The vegetables are a matter of choice but the principle is the
same.

Prepare vegetables, put in bowl, sprinkle liberally with coarse
salt and stand overnight; rinse, drain well and pack into jars; cover
with cold spiced vinegar, adding a couple of chillies and about 6
peppercorns per jar. Use a mixture of any of the following:

Cauliflowerettes, cucumber, green tomatoes, onions, shallots, green
beans, marrow, gherkins, celery [see also Piccalilli and End of Season
Relish (the last in the book)].

Mountain Ash Jelly *see Rowanberry Jelly.*

MULBERRY CHEESE

910g (2lb) mulberries, 150ml (¼ pint) water, sugar.

Put fruit in pan with water, simmer till tender, liquidize and/or
sieve; add 1kg sugar per kilogram pulp (1lb per lb), stirring till
dissolved; then boil till well thickened.

MULBERRY JAM

450g (1lb) mulberries, 150ml (¼ pint) water,
680g (1½lb) sugar, 1 lemon.

Put berries in pan with water; simmer till tender; add grated rind
and juice of lemon and sugar, stirring till dissolved; boil to set.
(The lemon may be omitted if preferred.)

MULBERRY JELLY

450g (1lb) mulberries, 150ml (¼ pint) water,
1 cooking apple, sugar.

Put berries in pan with water and cut up (but not peeled or cored)
apple; simmer till soft; strain through jelly bag; put juice in pan
with 800g sugar per litre liquid (1lb per pint), stirring till dissolved; boil rapidly to set; pot and cover at once.

MULBERRY AND APPLE JAM

Use equal quantities of mulberries and peeled, cored and chopped
apple, with 1kg sugar per kilogram fruit (1lb per lb) and prepare
as for mulberry jam.

MULBERRY AND APPLE JELLY

680g (1½lb) mulberries, 450g (1lb) cooking apples,
850ml (1½ pints) water, juice of 1 lemon.

Prepare as for Mulberry Jam, adding juice of lemon with the
sugar.

MUSHROOMS DRIED

The mushrooms must be fresh for this purpose and the method used depends largely on the weather.

Air Dried

Stalk mushrooms, wipe caps with damp cloth; using coarse darning needle and fine string or crochet thread, thread mushrooms carefully, knotting between each one and leaving enough string so that they do not touch; hang vertically or horizontally in a warm air current until completely dried, then store in airtight containers or brown paper bag.

Oven Dried

Stalk mushrooms, wipe with damp cloth and place on flat baking sheet without touching; leave in cool oven until absolutely dry; store as before.

In both cases, the stalks can be either oven-dried, or used up for immediate cooking.

MUSHROOMS PICKLED

Button Mushrooms

Small button mushrooms, salt, cayenne pepper, best vinegar.

Wipe mushrooms with damp cloth, place in fireproof dish, sprinkle with salt and cayenne and stand *beside* fire till moisture runs; (this can be done in very slow oven with the door ajar); when they have re-absorbed the moisture, add vinegar, simmer over very low heat for about 15 min but do not boil; pot and cover.

Field Mushrooms

450g (1lb) mushrooms, 2 blades mace, ½tsp. white pepper, 1tsp. salt, 1tsp. ground ginger, 1 very small finely chopped onion, vinegar.

Stalk and peel mushrooms; put in fireproof dish with onion, spices and sufficient vinegar just to cover; put in oven with lid on till slightly shrunk; transfer to jars, cover with hot vinegar and close down at once.

Just for the fun of it, I like the recipe dated 1767.

Boil your mushrooms in spring water and a little milk for about 12 min, then strain through a colander and throw into cold pump water where they must lie till cold. Get good vinegar and boil it in spices as mace, cloves, nutmeg. When it is cold, take your mushrooms out of the water, drain them dry and put into strained pickle. Distilled vinegar is best.

MUSHROOM POWDER

450g (1lb) mushrooms, 1 small onion, 3 cloves,
pinch of ground mace and white pepper.

Wipe mushrooms with damp cloth, put in heavy-based pan with other ingredients, and shake over medium heat until quite dry; you must keep the pan moving to prevent burning; transfer to flat tin and finish drying in very slow oven; pound to fine powder, put in small jars and seal. (A fine coffee grinder is very useful for this purpose.)

Mustard Pickle *see Piccalilli.*

N

NASTURTIUM SEEDS PICKLED

Nasturtium seeds, white vinegar, bay leaves, peppercorns, salt.

Put vinegar in pan with ½tsp. salt, 1 bay leaf and 3 peppercorns per 285ml (½ pint); boil, strain and allow to cool; pick seeds on a dry day, wash (remove any insects!), drain well; put in cool oven to dry; pack into jars, cover with cold vinegar and seal down; leave at least 3 months.

NASTURTIUM SAUCE

225g (½lb) nasturtium flowers, 570ml (1 pint) vinegar, 4 shallots, 3 cloves, ½tsp. salt, ¼tsp. cayenne pepper, Indian soy sauce.

Put flowers in large jar; simmer vinegar with spices, pour over flowers; cover closely and stand for 2 months; strain, add soy sauce to taste, then bottle and cork securely.

NUT HONEY

*28g (1oz) ground almonds, juice 3 oranges, grated rind of 1
orange, 28g (1oz) butter, 170g (6oz) sugar, 1 egg yolk.*

Put all together in double saucepan, stirring constantly, till mixture looks like honey; pot and cover at once.

NUTS

Nuts can be gathered from country hedges and then kept for Christmas. Keep them in a very dry place, shaking well from time to time and removing any pieces of dried leaf, etc. I use an old stone jar kept in a cupboard, and turn the nuts out about once a fortnight for a check over – it only takes about five minutes when tidying the cupboard.

O

ONIONS PICKLED

Small onions or shallots, salt, water, spiced vinegar.

Prepare bowl of brine [100g kitchen salt per litre water (2oz per pint)]; peel onions and leave in brine for at least 24 h; drain well, pack into jars and cover with cold spiced vinegar; close down tightly and leave at least 2 months before use. (If you have them on hand, 2 or 3 whole mustard seeds can be added to each jar.)

ONIONS SWEET PICKLED

As for pickled onions, adding 3½tsp. sugar per litre spiced vinegar (2tsp. per pint).

Onion and Apple Pickle *see under Apple*.
Onion and Cucumber Pickle *see under Cucumber*.

Onions are used in nearly every chutney or pickle and it is quite impossible to list all the recipes here since for the most part only about 225–450g (½–1lb) onions are involved. It is really a question of tying up onions with whatever else you have on hand, but see also Mixed Pickles, Piccalilli, End of Season Relish (p. 194).

Orange Cheese *see Orange Curd.*

ORANGE CHUTNEY

*4 oranges, 2 large cooking apples, 225g (½lb) brown sugar,
113g (4oz) raisins, 113g (4oz) preserved ginger, 14g (½oz)
chopped chillies, 1 onion, 28g (1oz) salt, 570ml
(1 pint) vinegar, pepper to taste.*

Peel oranges, remove pith and pips, cut up fruit; peel, core and finely chop apples and onions; put all together in pan with other ingredients, stirring from time to time and simmering till tender and thickened; pot and cover hot.

ORANGE CURD

*2 oranges, juice ½ lemon, 225g (½lb) sugar,
56g (2oz) butter, 4 eggs.*

Grate rind of oranges, squeeze and strain juice of oranges and lemon; beat eggs; melt butter in double saucepan, add all other ingredients, stirring constantly till thickened and near boiling point; pot and cover immediately.

ORANGE JELLY

910g (2lb) Seville oranges, 850ml (1½ pints) water,
680g (1½lb) lump sugar, water.

Squeeze juice from oranges, rough chop fruit and put all in pan
with water; bring to boil and simmer with lid on for about 2 h
or till peel is soft; strain through jelly bag; put juice in pan with
800g sugar per litre juice (1lb per pint), stirring till dissolved; boil
fast to set; pot and cover at once. (Sweet oranges can be used, but
it may be necessary to use commercial pectin to obtain a set.)

MARMALADE

Although the word 'marmalade' is used for a number of preserves, we most generally mean something in the nature of
oranges, grapefruit, etc., served at breakfast and hot over puddings. Even so, tastes are catholic – some people like it thick,
others finely sliced or minced. Below is a good basic recipe using
Seville oranges, followed by sweet oranges, and some variations
appear in this section and later in alphabetical order. The actual
preparation of the fruit is at personal discretion and the family's
preference.

SEVILLE ORANGE MARMALADE

910g (2lb) Seville oranges, 1 lemon, 1.8kg (4lb) sugar,
2.3l (4 pints) water.

Wash fruit, slice, coarse chop or mince as preferred; put in bowl
with water and pips in muslin bag; stand overnight; put in pan,
simmer gently till peel is soft and contents about halved; add

sugar, stirring till dissolved, boil fast to set; cool slightly before potting and covering.

SWEET ORANGE MARMALADE

4 sweet oranges, 4 lemons, 1 grapefruit, sugar,
2.3l (4 pints) water.

Wash fruit, put in pan with water and simmer for 20 min; remove fruit, cut in half and remove pips, then slice, chop or mince as desired; return to pan; allowing 1kg sugar per kilogram pulp (1lb per lb), stirring till dissolved; boil slowly for 45 min or to set.

ORANGE PEEL MARMALADE

170g (6oz) orange peel (sweet oranges), juice of 3 lemons,
1.1l (2 pints) water, 910g (2lb) sugar.

Follow basic recipe, chopping the peel and simmering in water till tender before adding lemon juice and sugar. This is a very good way of using up the peel of oranges used in a fresh fruit salad, etc.

ORANGE MARMALADE (Thick Dark)

910g (2lb) Seville oranges, 2 lemons, 1.8kg (4lb) sugar,
4tbs. black treacle, water.

Prepare fruit (thick chunks are best for this recipe); put in bowl with water to cover, and pips in muslin bag; stand overnight; put in pan, simmer till peel is tender, add sugar and black treacle, stirring till dissolved; then boil rapidly, stirring from time to time, to a thick set.

MARMALADES – FLAVOURED

Coriander – add 1tsp. crushed coriander per kilogram fruit
(½tsp. per pound) in the muslin bag with pips.

Mixed Spice – add 2tsp. per kilogram fruit (1tsp. per pound) at
the same time as the sugar.

Ginger – add 80g chopped crystallized ginger for every kilogram
oranges (1⅓oz per pound), at the same time as the sugar.

Brandy, sherry, whisky, liqueur – add 4tsp. per kilogram fruit
(2tsp. per pound) just before setting point.

ORANGE PASTE

Sweet oranges, caster sugar.

Soak oranges in water for 3 days, changing water every day; boil
whole till tender; put through liquidizer and/or sieve; put in pan
with 1kg sugar per kilogram pulp; beat well together over low
heat; put in jars while hot, sprinkle thickly with sugar, cover at
once; keeping time about 3 months.

ORANGE PICKLE

*6 very juicy oranges, 570ml (1 pint) white vinegar,
450g (1lb) sugar, 1tsp. each lemon peel, cinnamon,
mace and cloves (in muslin bag).*

Slice oranges thickly, remove pith and pips; put in double saucepan and steam till clear; in another pan put vinegar, sugar and bag
of spices and boil together for 10 min; remove spice bag, add fruit
and simmer slowly for 1 h; put in jars and seal at once.

To make a thicker syrup, remove orange rings to jars after simmering for 1 h; then boil syrup till thickened, cover orange rings,
and seal at once.

Do not use for at least 6 weeks.

Orange and Apple Chutney *see under Apple.*
Orange and Apricot Marmalade *see under Apricot.*
Orange and Banana Jam *see under Banana.*
Orange and Cranberry Conserve; Orange and Cranberry Relish
     see under Cranberry.
Orange and Date Chutney *see under Date.*
Orange and Fig Jam *see under Fig.*
Orange and Ginger Marmalade *see under Marmalades
     – flavoured.*
Orange and Gooseberry Jam *see under Gooseberry.*
Orange, Grapefruit and Lemon Marmalade *see Three-Fruit
     Marmalade.*

ORANGE AND LEMON CHUTNEY

*2 oranges, 3 lemons, 225g (½lb) onions, 450g (1lb) sugar,
170g (6oz) sultanas, 570ml (1 pint) spiced white vinegar (see
Vinegar, Spiced), 1tsp. each ground ginger and cinnamon.*

Wash fruit, squeeze juice, remove pith and pips and fine shred;
put in bowl with cold spiced vinegar; stand overnight; put in pan
with juices and finely sliced onion and simmer till tender; add
sultanas, spices and sugar, and cook till thickened, stirring from
time to time.

ORANGE AND LEMON CURD

Follow recipe for Lemon Curd, using juice and rind of 2 oranges,
the rind of 1 lemon, 113g (4oz) butter, 2 eggs and 225g (½lb)
sugar.

Orange and Lemon Jelly *see under Lemon.*

ORANGE AND LEMON MARMALADE

*4 Seville oranges, 1 sweet orange, 1 lemon, 1.8kg (4lb) sugar,
1.1l (2 pints) water.*

Procedure as for Seville Orange Marmalade.

Orange and Marrow Curd *see under Marrow.*
Orange and Pear Jam *see under Pear.*
Orange and Pumpkin Jam *see under Pumpkin.*
Orange and Rhubarb Jam *see under Rhubarb.*
Orange and Tomato Conserve *see under Tomato (Green).*

ORIENTAL CHUTNEY

*450g (1lb) dried apricots, 450g (1lb) dried peaches, 340g (¾lb)
stoned dates, 450g (1lb) sultanas, 340g (¾lb) seedless raisins,
340g (¾lb) currants, 1.4kg (3lb)Demerara sugar, 28g (1oz)
salt, 56g (2oz) garlic, 14g (½oz) each ground cloves and cinnamon, 570ml (1 pint) vinegar, water.*

Chop apricots, peaches and dates; put in pan with remaining
fruit and water just to cover; simmer slowly till tender; add vinegar, spices and sugar, stirring till dissolved; boil fast for about 30
min, stirring frequently, until thick; taste, add salt as required; pot
hot and do not use for 6 months.

P

PARADISE JELLY

450g (1lb) apples, 450g (1lb) quinces,
225g (½lb) cranberries, sugar, water.

Wash and quarter apples and quinces, removing seeds from the latter; put in pan with cranberries and water just to cover; simmer till tender; strain through jelly bag; put juice in pan with 800g sugar per litre liquid (1lb per pint), stirring till dissolved, then boil fast to set; pot and cover at once.

PARSLEY HONEY

140g (5oz) parsley (including stalks), 850ml (1½ pints) water,
450g (1lb) sugar, 1tsp. white vinegar.

Wash parsley and dry well; rough chop; put in pan in boiling water till reduced to 570ml (1 pint); add sugar, stirring till dissolved, boil 20 mins; add vinegar, stirring well; pot and cover immediately.

PARSLEY JELLY

340g (12oz) parsley, 5 lemons, sugar, water, green colouring.

Put parsley in pan with water just to cover and the chopped peel of 1 lemon; boil for 1 h; strain; put liquid in pan with juice of the 5 lemons and 800g sugar per litre liquid (1lb per pint), stirring till dissolved; boil till nearly set, add a few drops of green colouring; boil to set; pot and cover at once.

PASSION FRUIT JAM

Passion fruit, sugar, lemon.

Scoop pulp from fruit, put in pan with juice of 2 lemons and 800g sugar per litre pulp (1lb per pint); stir till sugar dissolved; boil fast to set.

As fresh grenadillas (or passion fruit) are not often available in England, you can make this jam, with tinned fruit:

Canned passion fruit, sugar, lemon.

Pulp fruit, and if already sweetened use only 400g sugar per litre pulp (½lb sugar per pint) and continue as above.

PEAS DRIED

Shell young peas (use pods for soup); blanch in boiling water for 3 min; drain well, spread on trays on thick muslin till really dry; (change muslin from time to time to assist drying); store in airtight jars.

PEASE FOR CHRISTMAS (1799)

Shell fine young pease, put in some boiling water with some salt, after boiling 5 min, drain in colander and put in cloth doubled five or six times. Let them hang free in the air to dry. Fill pease into clean and dry jars, put on top some mutton fat and let them be put in a cool dry closet. Pease done this way will keep good for Christmas.

TO PICKLE GREEN PEASE (OR BEANS) 1677

Take water and vinegar, boil well, just scald the pease or beans and put in close earthenware vessel. When you have a mind to, boil them. Steep them a night in fresh water and when they be boiled they will eat almost as if new gathered, which has been proved to the admiration of many who have wondered where such delicacies could be had in the dead of winter.

PEACH BUTTER

Follow recipe for Apricot Butter.

PEACHES BRANDIED

Peaches, sugar, brandy.

Skin peaches, put in jar with good layers of sugar between and when jar is full add 570ml (1 pint) brandy; cover closely over tight muslin; keep very cool; peaches may be left whole, or halved and stoned.

PEACH CHUTNEY

910g (2lb) peaches, 450g (1lb) onions, 170g (6oz) stoned raisins, 225g (½lb) soft brown sugar, ½tsp, dry mustard, ½tsp. chilli powder, 1tsp. salt, 285ml (½ pint) vinegar, grated rind and juice of 1 small orange and 1 small lemon, ½tsp. turmeric, ¼tsp. cinnamon.

Wash and stone peaches, put in pan with fine chopped onions and raisins; add remaining ingredients; bring to boil, stirring gently; simmer very slowly for 1½–2 h or until thick, stirring from time to time.

PEACH CONSERVE

450g (1lb) peaches, 450g (1lb) sugar, juice 1 lemon.

Put quartered and stoned peaches into pan with sugar and lemon juice; cook very slowly till sugar is dissolved, stirring constantly; boil gently to set.

PEACH JAM (Dried Fruit)

450g (1lb) dried peaches, 1.4kg (3lb) preserving sugar,
1.7l (3 pints) water.

Follow method of Dried Apricot Jam.

PEACH JAM (Fresh Fruit)

910g (2lb) fresh peaches, 910g (2lb) sugar,
150ml (¼ pint) water, juice of 1 lemon.

Follow method as for Fresh Apricot Jam.

PEACH MARMALADE

As for Apricot Marmalade.

PEACHES PICKLED (Dried Fruit)

450g (1lb) dried peaches, 1.4kg (3lb) sugar, 2.3l (4 pints)
white vinegar, 1 blade mace, 1 small stick cinnamon, 6 cloves.

Put peaches in large bowl, cover with vinegar; stand 48 h; put into pan, bring to boil, add sugar, stirring till dissolved; add spices, continue to boil till fruit is transparent and tender; remove peaches, draining well and when cool pack into jars; continue boiling syrup till it thickens then pour over fruit and cover closely.

PEACHES PICKLED (Fresh Fruit) (1)

450g (1lb) peaches, 225g (½lb) sugar, 425ml (¾ pint) wine or cider vinegar, 14g (½oz) mixed spice.

Peel peaches; put in pan with sugar, vinegar and spices; bring slowly to boil, simmer 5 min; remove fruit carefully to warmed jars; simmer syrup till it thickens; pour over fruit and cover closely.

PEACHES PICKLED (Fresh Fruit) (2)

6 peaches (just under-ripe), 1.7l (3 pints) water, 225g (½lb) salt, 1.1l (2 pints) vinegar, 28g (1oz) ground ginger, 1 blade mace, 28g (1oz) mixed spice, 56g (2oz) sugar.

Rub peaches with damp cloth; put in pan with salt and water; boil for 2 min; remove peaches, skin, put in bowl and cover with water in which boiled; stand for 3 days; drain well; boil vinegar with spices; add peaches and simmer for 10 min; remove fruit carefully to jar(s), pour over hot pickled vinegar and cover closely.

Peach, Apple and Carrot Marmalade *see under Carrot.*

PEACH AND PEAR CONSERVE

450g (1lb) peaches, 450g (1lb) firm pears, 150ml (¼ pint) water, grated rind and juice of 2 lemons, 910g (2lb) sugar.

Peel, stone and quarter peaches; peel, core and cube pears; 450g (1lb) weight of each when prepared; put water, grated lemon rind and sugar in pan and boil to thick syrup; add lemon juice, peaches and pears; simmer gently till fruit is transparent and syrup sets firmly.

PEACH AND PEAR JAM

*450g (1lb) peaches and firm pears (when prepared), 150ml (¼
pint) water, grated rind and juice of 2 lemons,
910g (2lb) sugar.*

Quarter prepared peaches and cube prepared pears; put in pan
with water and simmer gently till tender but not pulped; add
grated rind and juice of lemon and sugar, stirring till dissolved;
boil fast to set.

PEACH AND PINEAPPLE MARMALADE

*1.1kg (2½lb) dried peaches, 1 large tin drained pineapple
chunks, 4l (7 pints) water, 2 lemons, 2.7kg (6lb) sugar.*

Put peaches in bowl with water and stand for 24 h; put in pan and
cook slowly till tender; remove fruit and rough chop; return to
pan with strained lemon juice and grated rind, pineapple chunks
and sugar; boil fast to set.

PEACH AND RASPBERRY JAM

*910g (2lb) skinned and stoned fresh peaches, 910g (2lb)
raspberries, 150ml (¼ pint) water, 1.4kg (3lb) sugar.*

Slice peaches; crack some of the stones to obtain kernels; put all
fruit, water and kernels into pan and cook slowly till tender; add
sugar, stirring till dissolved; boil 15–20 min, stirring occasionally,
till set.

Peaches *see also Fruit Cockaigne, Mixed Fruit Jam, Mixed Fruit
Pickle.*

PEAR CHUTNEY (1)

*1.4kg (3lb) firm pears, 450g (1lb) onions, grated rind and juice
of 1 lemon, and 1 orange, 225g (½lb) sugar, 225g (½lb) seedless raisins, 285ml (½ pint) vinegar, 1tsp. each salt and ground
ginger, ½tsp. ground cloves.*

Peel, core and slice pears; chop onions; put together in pan with
all other ingredients; bring slowly to boil; simmer gently for
about 2 h until thick and smooth.

PEAR CHUTNEY (2)

*680g (1½lb) pears (when peeled and cored), 225g (½lb)
onions, 225g (½lb) green tomatoes, 113g (4oz) stoned raisins,
113g (4oz) celery, 340g (¾lb) Demerara sugar, ¼tsp. cayenne
pepper and ground ginger, 1tsp. salt, 570ml (1 pint) malt
vinegar, 6 peppercorns.*

Peel, core and slice pears, chop onions, slice tomatoes; chop raisins
and celery; put all ingredients, except sugar, in pan and simmer
gently till tender; add sugar and continue cooking till thickened,
stirring from time to time.

PEAR HONEY

Pears, sugar, water.

Take off blossom end of small pears; quarter fruit and put in pan with water to cover; simmer till very soft; strain through jelly bag; put juice in pan with 600g sugar per litre liquid (¾lb per pint) and bring to boil; simmer to thin syrup.

PEAR MARMALADE

Follow recipe for Apple Marmalade using peeled and quartered pears.

PEARS PICKLED

Small firm pears, 570ml (1 pint) distilled white vinegar, 910g (2lb) sugar, 14g (½oz) clove, rind of ½ lemon, 14g (½oz) root ginger, 50mm (2in) cinnamon stick, 1 bay leaf.

Remove stalks from fruit; put vinegar, sugar and spices (tied in muslin bag) in pan; stir till sugar dissolved; add pears; simmer till just tender; remove fruit carefully to warmed jars; remove spice bag and bring syrup to boil; pour over fruit and cover closely.

PEAR PRESERVE

1.4kg (3lb) pears, 425ml (¾ pint) water, rind of 1½ lemons, 3 tbs lemon juice, 570g (1¼lb) sugar.

Peel, core, and cut pears into chunks; thinly pare rind of lemons and put in pan with water and the peel and cores of the pears; simmer about 10 min then strain; put pear chunks in pan with strained liquid and lemon juice; simmer till tender; add sugar, stirring till dissolved; bring to boil then boil fast to set.

PEARS SPICED

There is so little difference between this type of recipe and pickled pears that only one recipe is being included.

PEAR AND APPLE JAM

*450g (1lb) stewing pears (peeled and cored), 450g (1lb) cook-
ing apples (peeled and cored), 910g (2lb) sugar, 2 lemons.*

Slice fruit and put in layers in bowl with sugar and grated rind of
lemon; squeeze juice of lemons and pour over; stand overnight;
put in pan, bring very slowly to the boil, stirring till sugar is dissolved, boil fast till it thickens.

Pear, Apple and Plum Marmalade *see under Plum.*

PEAR AND CLOVE JAM

Follow recipe for Apple and Clove Jam, using firm pears instead
of apples.

PEAR AND GINGER JAM

Follow recipe for Apple and Ginger Jam, using pears instead of
apples; if the pears are hard, it may be necessary to allow extra
cooking time before adding sugar.

PEAR AND GINGER PRESERVE

*450g (1lb) pears, 450g (1lb) sugar, 56g (2oz) preserved ginger,
juice 2 lemons, 285ml (½ pint) water.*

Peel and core pears; cut in long slices; cut ginger into small
chunks; put water and sugar in pan, stirring till dissolved; add

fruit, ginger and lemon juice; cook very slowly till tender; carefully remove fruit to warmed jars; boil syrup for further 5 min; pour over fruit and seal down.

PEAR AND LEMON JAM

Follow recipe for Apple Lemon Jam substituting pears for apples.

PEAR AND ORANGE JAM

450g (1lb) cooking pears (when peeled and cored), 150ml (¼ pint) water, 450g (1lb) sugar, grated rind and juice of 2 oranges.

Cut up peeled and cored pears; tie cores, etc., in muslin bag; put in pan with water and simmer very slowly till soft and pulpy; remove muslin bag; using wooden spoon mash pulp till smooth, add sugar, stirring till dissolved, then the rind and juice of the oranges; bring to boil, stirring constantly for about 10 min or till thick.

Pear and Peach Conserve *see under Peach.*
Pear and Peach Jam *see under Peach.*

PEAR AND PINEAPPLE CONSERVE

1.4kg (3lb) pears, 1 x 450g (1 x 1lb) can pineapple chunks, 1 orange, sugar.

Peel, core and cube pears; put in bowl with pineapple, grated rind and juice of orange and for each 1kg (1lb) add ¾kg (¾lb) sugar; stand overnight; remove to pan, heat slowly, stirring to dissolve sugar; simmer till thick; pot and cover at once.

As an added flavour, halve 12 maraschino cherries at the end of cooking, and stir in well with a little of their juice.

PEAR AND PINEAPPLE JAM SPICED

1.4kg (3lb) cooking pears, 225g (½lb) crushed pineapple, 1 orange, 1 lemon, 910g (2lb) sugar, 4 cloves, 150-mm (6-in) stick cinnamon, 25-mm (1-in) ginger root.

Peel, core and rough chop pears; wash and rough chop orange and lemon, discarding pips; put all together in pan with spices in muslin bag, stirring till sugar is dissolved; boil for about 30 min or until thick.

Pear and Quince Chutney *see under Quince.*

PEPPER CHUTNEY (Sweet)

450g (1lb) green peppers, 450g (1lb) red peppers, 225g (½lb) onions, 425ml (¾ pint) white vinegar, 28g (1oz) salt, 170g (6oz) sugar pieces.

Wash peppers, cut in slices removing seeds and pith, then chop; blanch in boiling water for 3 min, cool and drain; put in pan with all other ingredients, stirring till sugar is dissolved; simmer slowly, stirring occasionally, till mixture thickens.

PEPPER CHUTNEY (Red)

2 red peppers, 1 aubergine, 1 large cooking apple, 28g (1oz) brown sugar, 1 clove garlic, ½tsp. saffron, 113g (4oz) onions, ½tsp. curry powder and ground ginger, 3 chillies, 285ml (½ pint) spiced vinegar (see Vinegars).

Seed and slice peppers, peel, core and slice apple, finely slice aubergine and onions; put all ingredients in pan over gentle heat;

cook till vegetables are tender and mixture thickens, stirring occasionally.

PEPPER (Green) AND APPLE CHUTNEY

*3 green peppers, 1.4kg (3lb) sharp apples, 1medium onion,
225g (8oz) raisins, 1½tbs. ground ginger,
113g (4oz) redcurrant jelly.*

Seed and pith peppers and mince or chop finely with peeled and cored apples, onion and raisins; put in pan with all other ingredients, stirring till sugar is dissolved; simmer gently for 1 h or until thick.

Pepper and Aubergine Chutney *see under Aubergine; also Red Pepper Chutney above.*

PEPPERS CABBAGE FILLED

*6 peppers (red or green), ½ head white cabbage, ½tsp. salt, 1tbs.
mustard seed, 570ml (1 pint) vinegar.*

Cut peppers in half, remove seeds and pith, but keep shells intact; very finely shred cabbage and mix well with salt and mustard seed; pack tightly into peppers, fasten halves tightly together with toothpicks or coarse cotton; stand upright in jar; covered with cold spiced vinegar and store in a cool place.

PEPPER PHILADELPHIA RELISH

*450g (1lb) green peppers, 225g (½lb) red peppers, 680g (1½lb)
drumhead cabbage, 113g (¼lb) celery, 1tbs. salt, mustard seed
and brown sugar, 285ml (½ pint) vinegar.*

Cut and seed peppers, mince all vegetables together, put into basin, sprinkle with salt; stand overnight; drain throroughly and pack into jar; put vinegar in pan with sugar and mustard seed, bring to boil and pour hot over vegetables and cover tightly. (This relish does not keep but is ideal made some days before a barbecue or similar.)

PICCALILLI

Once again, this is a pickle for which there are many variations – of the twenty-odd I have studied no two had identical ingredients, but the principle is always the same:

Prepare vegetables, put in brine [100g salt to 1litre water (2oz per pint)] and stand overnight; put vinegar in pan, using a little to mix dry mustard, etc., to a paste, add all other spices and sugar where used; simmer together till slightly thick; drain vegetables well, pack into jars and cover with the hot mixture; cover tightly.

(1) *2 onions, 3 tomatoes, 1 cauliflower, 225g (½lb) shallots, 225g (½lb) gherkins, 1.1l (2 pints) vinegar, salt, 14g (½oz) whole peppers and ground ginger, 28g (1oz) dry mustard, 1tsp. ground cloves.*

(2) *1.4kg (3lb) marrow, 450g (1lb) cauliflower, 340g (¾lb) green beans, 225g (½lb) onions (all weighed when prepared), ½ large cucumber, 170g (6oz) sugar, 1.1l (2 pints) vinegar, 42g (1½oz) dry mustard and ground ginger, 340g (¾lb) salt (for brine), 21g (¾oz) flour, 14g (½oz) turmeric.*

(3) *910g (2lb) any mixed vegetables, 570ml (1 pint) vinegar, 56g (2oz) sugar, 1tbs. dry mustard, 14g (½oz) turmeric, ground ginger, flour or cornflour (the latter makes a thicker sauce), 28g (1oz) pickling spice, brine as before.*

Piccalilli Sweet *see recipe (2) above.*

PICKLE SWEET

Follow recipe for Piccalilli (2) leaving out dry mustard, turmeric and ginger.

PILCHARDS PICKLED

This is rather an odd man out in this book but they really are so useful in the summer that it just had to be included.

Pilchards, vinegar, water, bay leaves, peppercorns, cloves, salt.

Remove heads, clean fish and scale them; wash well; stand in stone jar; allow equal quantities of vinegar and water to fill, with 3½ bay leaves, 10 peppercorns, 3½ cloves and 2tsp. salt per litre liquid; stand jar in slow to moderate oven for 1½–2 h; remove and seal down tightly.

PINEAPPLE BRANDIED

*910g (2lb) fresh pineapple, 150ml (¼ pint) brandy, 3 cloves,
50mm (2in) cinnamon stick, water, 84g (3oz) sugar.*

Cut pineapple into large cubes, put in pan with 285ml (½ pint) water, simmer till just tender; remove pineapple, add sugar with cinnamon and spices; simmer till syrupy; add pineapple, simmer for 10 min; remove from heat, add brandy, stirring in well; when cool remove fruit to jar, cover with syrup and seal down. (This recipe can be made with a 910g (2lb) can of pineapple pieces, draining and using juice to simmer with sugar and spices till syrupy and continue as before.)

PINEAPPLE JAM

910g (2lb) pineapple (when prepared), 680g (1½lb) sugar,
150ml (¼ pint) water.

Peel pineapple, remove hard core, cut in cubes; do this on a plate to catch as much juice as possible; put sugar and water in pan, simmer till dissolved and just syruping, add pineapple, cook to set.

PINEAPPLE JELLY

1large can pineapple juice 570 g (20 oz), 1tsp. lemon juice,
1.1kg (2½lb) sugar, 1 bottle commercial pectin.

Put sugar, lemon and pineapple juice in pan, stirring till sugar is dissolved; bring to fast boil; add pectin, fast boil for further ½ min, skimming if necessary; pot and cover at once.

PINEAPPLE MARMALADE (1)

1large tin pineapple, 3 Jaffa oranges, 1 lemon, 1.8kg (4lb)
sugar, 570ml (1 pint) water.

Wash, peel and shred peel of oranges and lemon; cut fruit into pieces, put in bowl with pineapple juice and water; stand over-night; put all in pan, simmer till tender; add pineapple chunks and sugar, stirring till dissolved, cook for about ¾ h; pot and cover when cold.

PINEAPPLE MARMALADE (2) (Very Quick)

1 tin crushed pineapple, 56g (2oz) dark brown sugar.

Put all together in pan on medium heat, stirring constantly till mixture thickens. (This can be used as pickle by adding 1tsp. mixed spice during the cooking.)

PINEAPPLE RELISH

*225g (½lb) crushed fresh pineapple, 56g (2oz) onion,
56g (2oz) butter, 28g (1oz) chopped fresh parsley,
28g (1oz) dry mustard.*

Chop onions, put in pan with butter and cook till soft but not brown, add remaining ingredients and mix well together. (This recipe is not for keeping, but it is useful when something unusual is required quickly and is absolutely delicious with cold pork or ham.)

Pineapple and Apple Jam *see under Apple.*
Pineapple and Apricot Jam *see under Apricot.*

PINEAPPLE AND APRICOT PRESERVE

*1 medium pineapple, 450g (1lb) dried apricots, juice and rind
of 3 lemons, 1.8kg (4lb) sugar, water.*

Peel pineapple and cut in cubes; do this on plate to catch as much juice as possible; make juice up to 1.7l (3 pints) with water and put in bowl with washed apricots; stand overnight; put in pan with lemon juice, simmer till tender; add crushed pineapple, grated lemon rind and sugar, stirring till dissolved; bring to boil and cook for about 10 min or to set.

Pineapple and Banana Jam *see under Banana*.
Pineapple and Blackberry Jam *see under Blackberry*.
Pineapple and Blackcurrant Jam *see under Blackcurrant*.
Pineapple and Cherry Preserve *see under Cherry*.
Pineapple and Lemon Preserve *see under Lemon*.
Pineapple and Marrow Jam *see under Marrow*.
Pineapple and Melon Jam *see under Melon*.

PINEAPPLE AND MINT JELLY

1 tin sweetened pineapple juice, 340g (¾lb) sugar, juice of 3 lemons, 28g (1oz) fresh chopped mint.

Put pineapple juice in pan, bring to boil, add lemon juice and sugar, stirring till dissolved; boil to setting point rapidly, add chopped mint, stir in well; pot and cover immediately.

Pineapple and Peach Marmalade *see under Peach*.
Pineapple and Pear Conserve; Pineapple and Pear Jam *see under Pear*.

PLUM CHEESE

450g (1lb) plums, 450g (1lb) sugar, 70ml (⅛ pint) water.

Slit plums (after washing); put in pan with water; simmer very gently till tender; remove stones; put through liquidizer and/or sieve; put in pan with sugar, stirring till dissolved; boil fast to set.

PLUM CHUTNEY

Yet another preserve that has many variations but with basic cooking principles: Stone the plums, put in pan with any other fruit and/or prepared vegetables and half the vinegar; simmer till tender, add remaining ingredients; simmer till thickened.

(1) *910g (2lb) purple plums, 910g (2lb) cooking apples, 450g (1lb) Spanish onions, 285ml (½ pint) cider vinegar, 450g (1lb) sugar (granulated), 450g (1lb) brown sugar, 14g (½oz) allspice and ground cloves, 28g (1oz) salt, cayenne pepper to taste.*

(2) *910g (2lb) plums, 225g (½lb) apples, 340g (¾lb) brown sugar, 450g (1lb) raisins, 14g (½oz) garlic, 14g (½oz) ground ginger, 3 dried chillies, 570ml (1 pint) vinegar.*

(3) *680g (1½lb) plums, 225g (½lb) apples, 113g (¼lb) brown sugar, 225g (½lb) onions, 225g (½lb) sultanas, 425ml (¾ pint) vinegar, 14g (½oz) salt, ½tsp. each allspice, cinnamon and ground ginger, cayenne pepper to taste.*

(4) *450g (1lb) plums, 150ml (¼ pint) vinegar, 170g (6oz) sugar, 56g (2oz) sultanas, ½tsp. salt and ground ginger, 14g (½oz) pickling spice in muslin bag.*

(5) *680g (1½lb) plums, 225g (½lb) apples, 225g (½lb) sugar, 570ml (1 pint) vinegar, 225g (½lb) onions, 113g (4oz) stoned raisins, 113g (4oz) sliced carrots, 28g (1oz) salt, 1tsp. each ground cloves, cinnamon, ginger and allspice.*

PLUM CONSERVE

450g (1lb) plums, 450g (1lb) sugar,
56g (2oz) stoned raisins, 56g (2oz) walnuts.

Stone plums, put in pan with raisins; simmer very gently till tender, add sugar, stirring till dissolved; boil fast to set, add walnuts and stir in well.

PLUM CONSERVE (Mixed Plums)

450g (1lb) each golden, red and Victoria plums,
1.4kg (3lb) sugar, 150ml (¼ pint) water.

Stone plums, simmer red and golden plums in water till softened, then add the Victorias; simmer till all are tender; add sugar, stirring till dissolved; boil fast to set.

PLUM CONSERVE (Victoria Plums)

Follow recipe for Plum Conserve, omitting raisins and walnuts, but if liked a few kernels from the stones may be added at the end of cooking.

PLUM JAM

450g (1lb) plums (when stoned), 450g (1lb) sugar, water.

Put stoned plums, halved, into pan with very little water to prevent catching and simmer till tender; add sugar, stirring till dissolved; boil slowly to set. (A few kernels from the stones can be added at the end if liked.)

PLUM JAM (Victoria Plums)

Follow recipe for Plum Jam (Whole Fruit) below, adding as many kernels as possible at the end.

PLUM JAM (Whole Fruit)

450g (1lb) plums (when stoned), 450g (1lb) sugar.

Put stoned plums in bowl, sprinkle with sugar; stand overnight; put in pan, heat very slowly, stirring till sugar is dissolved, then boil gently to set.

PLUM JELLY

Ripe plums, sugar, water.

Wash plums, put in pan, half-covering with water; put lid on pan and cook very slowly till fruit breaks (this can be done in fireproof dish in oven very slowly); strain through jelly bag; return juice to pan with 800g sugar per litre liquid (1lb per pint), stirring till dissolved, then boil fast for 30 min or to set; pot and cover immediately. (A few drops of cochineal can be added if colour is pale.)

PLUM JELLY (Victoria Plums)

*Victoria plums, lemon, sugar, 300ml water per
kilogram fruit (½ pint per 2lb).*

Follow recipe for Plum Jelly, allowing juice of 2 lemons and 800g sugar per litre juice (1 lemon, 1lb sugar per pint).

Plum Marmalade *follow recipe for Apricot Marmalade.*

PLUMS PICKLED

*910g (2lb) plums, 450g (1lb) Demerara sugar, cloves,
stick cinnamon, 285ml (½ pint) best vinegar.*

Choose slightly under-ripe plums; stick a clove in one end and a small piece of cinnamon in the other end; put in fireproof dish with sugar and vinegar, cover and put in moderate oven till it reaches boiling point; take out and stand till next day; remove fruit carefully to jars; boil liquid gently for 30 min, pour over fruit; cover when cold.

PLUMS SPICED

Plums, cloves, stick cinnamon, brown sugar,
wine vinegar, water, coarse salt.

Prick plums all over with needle or toothpick; pack into jars with a clove between each layer; half-way up the jar put in a 37-mm (1½-in) stick of cinnamon, and another one on the top layer; make a syrup of 850ml (1½ pints) wine vinegar, 285ml (½ pint) water, 680g (1½lb) brown sugar and 2tsp. salt (or proportions thereof); pour hot over plums; cover at once, do not use for at least 8 weeks. (An added flavour is given if a fresh raspberry leaf is put in with each layer of plums.)

Plum and Apple Cheese *see under Apple.*

PLUM AND APPLE CHUTNEY

910g (2lb) plums (when stoned), 450g (1lb) sharp apples
(peeled and cored), 450g (1lb) shallots, 450g (1lb) raisins,
170g (6oz) Demerara sugar, 1tsp. each ground ginger and
allspice, ¼tsp. each ground cloves, nutmeg, cayenne pepper and
dry mustard, 28g (1oz) salt, 570ml (1 pint) vinegar.

Chop apples and onions, put in pan with plums and all other ingredients; bring to boil, stirring, then simmer till thickened, stirring occasionally.

PLUM AND APPLE JAM

910g (2lb) plums (stoned), 450g (1lb) sharp apples (peeled and cored), 150ml (¼ pint) water, 1.4kg (3lb) sugar.

Put fruit in pan with water; simmer till soft; add sugar, stirring till dissolved; boil to set.

Plum and Apple Jelly *see under Apple.*

PLUM AND PEAR MARMALADE

450g (1lb) Victoria plums, 450g (1lb) apples, 450g (1lb) pears, 1kg (2¼lb) sugar.

Stone, peel and halve plums; peel, core and cut up apples and pears; put all together in pan with sugar on low heat, bringing slowly to boil, stirring till sugar dissolved; cook gently to set.

Plum and Marrow Jam *see under Marrow.*
Plums *see also Mixed Fruit Jam, Mixed Fruit Pickle.*

PRUNE CHUTNEY

450g (1lb) prunes, 285ml (½ pint) vinegar, 340g (¾lb) sugar, ½tsp. cinnamon and cloves.

Soak prunes overnight; simmer in same water; drain, keeping liquid; stone and cut up prunes; return to pan with liquid and all other ingredients and simmer till thick.

PRUNE CONSERVE

450g (1lb) small prunes, 570ml (1 pint) water,
450g (1lb) sugar, juice 2 lemons.

Soak prunes overnight; simmer in same water till soft; take out fruit, remove stones, return to pan and weigh; for each kilogram (1lb) pulp add juice of 2 (1) lemons and 800g (1lb) sugar, stirring till dissolved; boil fast to set.

PRUNE MARMALADE

680g (1½lb) prunes, 1 lemon, 450g (1lb) sugar,
850ml (1½ pints) water.

Soak prunes overnight; simmer in same water till tender; remove stones; very thinly slice lemons, removing pips and centre pith; add to prunes with sugar, stirring till dissolved; boil gently till thick.

PRUNE PRESERVE

Follow recipe for Prune Conserve, adding grated rind of 1 orange when simmering prunes and 170g (6oz) chopped walnuts at setting point.

PRUNES SPICED

450g (1lb) prunes, 425ml (¾ pint) vinegar, 225g (½lb) sugar,
1½tsp. mixed spice, cold tea.

Soak prunes overnight in cold tea to cover; remove to pan, simmer till soft, drain, keeping 570ml (1 pint) liquid; boil together vinegar, sugar, spices and juice from prunes; pack fruit into jar, pour over syrup; cover when cold.

PRUNE AND NUT CHUTNEY

*450g (1lb) prunes, 340g (¾lb) cooking apples (when peeled
and cored), 280g (10oz) dark brown sugar, 285ml (½ pint)
wine vinegar, 113g (¼lb) hazelnuts, 1tsp. each curry powder,
cinnamon and allspice, pinch of cayenne.*

Wash prunes, cover with boiling water; stand overnight; fine
chop apples, simmer with little sugar till soft; remove prune
stones and chop fruit; add to apple with all other ingredients;
boil for about 45 min, stirring constantly, until thickened; pot
and cover at once.

Prunes *see also Dried Fruit Pickle.*

PUMPKIN JAM

*1.4kg (3lb) pumpkin (when prepared), 56g (2oz) root ginger,
1.4kg (3lb) sugar, grated rind and juice 2 lemons.*

Boil peeled and cubed pumpkin till tender; drain well; mash; add
grated rind and juice of lemon with bruised ginger in muslin
bag; bring to boil, add sugar, stirring till dissolved; boil gently till
thick, about 20 min.

PUMPKIN PICKLED AND SPICED

*1.1. kg (2½lb) pumpkin (when prepared), 570ml (1 pint)
vinegar, 910g (2lb) sugar, ½tsp. cloves (whole),
50-mm (2-in) stick cinnamon.*

Put vinegar in pan with sugar and spices tied in muslin bag, bring
to boil, boil 5 min; add pumpkin; cook very slowly till tender;
remove pumpkin to jars; cover with syrup; close down at once.

Pumpkin and Apple Jam *see under Apple.*

PUMPKIN AND CRANBERRY JAM

*1.6 kg (3½lb) pumpkin (when prepared), 225g (½lb) cranberries,
1.8kg (4lb) sugar, 570ml (1 pint) water, 1tsp. tartaric acid.*

Simmer diced pumpkin with cranberries, water and tartaric acid
till tender; add sugar, stirring till dissolved; boil steadily for about
20 min until thickened.

PUMPKIN AND LEMON JAM

Follow recipe for Pumpkin Jam, leaving out ginger and using 3
instead of 2 lemons.

PUMPKIN AND ORANGE JAM

Follow recipe for Pumpkin Jam, using 1 lemon and 3 oranges
(grated rind, juice *and* pulp).

Pumpkin and Quince Jam *see under Quince.*

The time to use Pumpkin is at Hallowe'en when the children
want a scooped-out pumpkin for their fun – then you can get
someone to do the hard work for you!

Q

QUINCE CHEESE

Quinces, sugar, lemon, water.

Chop fruit; simmer in very little water till soft; liquidize and/or sieve; put in pan with 1kg sugar per kilogram pulp (1lb per lb), stirring till dissolved; boil fast to set.

QUINCE JAM

450g (1lb) quinces, 450g (1lb) sugar, juice ½ lemon.

Peel, core and chop fruit; simmer in very little water till tender; add lemon juice and sugar, stirring gently till dissolved, boil fast to set.

QUINCE JELLY

Quinces, sugar, water.

Cut up fruit, put in pan with sufficient water to float the fruit; boil till pulpy; strain through jelly bag; put juice in pan with 800g sugar per litre liquid (1lb per pint), stirring till dissolved; boil about 45 min to setting point, skimming as necessary; pot and cover at once. [If fruit is very ripe, add juice of 2 lemons per litre liquid (1 lemon per pint) at the same time as the sugar.]

QUINCE MARMALADE

Peel, core and cut up fruit small; put peelings and cores in pan with water to cover, boil for 3 min; strain and cool; put fruit and liquid in pan, simmer gently till just tender; add sugar, stirring till dissolved; cook gently till syrup sets.

QUINCE PRESERVE

910g (2lb) quinces, 910g (2lb) parsnips, 1 lemon, 1 orange,
1.1l (2 pints) water, sugar.

Wash and slice parsnips, put in pan with lemon and orange finely sliced; simmer till soft; strain; put liquid in pan with peeled, cored and sliced quinces with equal weight of sugar, stirring till dissolved; cook gently till fruit is tender; remove fruit to jars; reduce liquid to thick syrup, pour over fruit; cover when cold.

QUINCE AND APPLE JAM

Follow recipe for Quince Jam, using 450g (1lb) quinces, 450g (1lb) peeled and cored apples, 150ml (¼ pint) water, 910g (2lb) sugar.

QUINCE AND APPLE JELLY

Follow recipe for Quince Jelly, using 450g (1lb) quinces and 450g (1lb) apples.

QUINCE AND CRANBERRY PRESERVE

6 quinces, 340g (¾lb) cranberries, 425ml (¾ pint) water, 1.1kg (2½lb) sugar.

Peel, core and cut up quinces, put in pan with water, simmer till soft; put through coarse sieve, return to pan with cranberries; simmer 15 min till cranberries are tender, add sugar, stirring till dissolved; cook gently about 20 min or to set.

Quince, Apple and cranberry jelly *see Paradise Jelly*.

QUINCE AND MARROW JAM

1.8kg (4lb) quinces, 910g (2lb) prepared marrow, 1.8kg (4lb) sugar, 1.1l (2 pints) water.

Peel, core and slice quinces, cube marrow; put together in pan with water; simmer till pulped, add sugar, stirring till dissolved; bring to boil and cook for about 10 min or to set.

QUINCE AND PEAR CHUTNEY

450g (1lb) quinces, 910g (2lb) cooking pears, 450g (1lb) onions, 450g (1lb) green tomatoes, 225g (½lb) stoned raisins, 225g (½lb) celery, 680g (1½lb) Demerara sugar, 1.1l (2 pints) vinegar, 1tsp. grated horseradish, ½tsp. ground ginger, 7g (¼oz) salt, ¼tsp. cayenne pepper, 5 peppercorns.

Peel, core and cut up quinces and pears, wash tomatoes, skin onions and put all through mincer together with raisins; put in covered pan, simmering very gently till tender; add all remaining ingredients, tying peppercorns and horseradish in muslin bag; cook very slowly, stirring from time to time, until thickened – probably 3–4 h; cool before potting.

QUINCE AND PUMPKIN JAM

450g (1lb) quinces (when prepared), 1.1kg (2½lb) pumpkin (when prepared), 570ml (1 pint) water, 1.6 kg (3½lb) sugar, 1tsp. tartaric acid.

Dice prepared fruit, put in pan with water and tartaric acid; bring to boil, cook gently for about 30 min till tender; add sugar, stirring till dissolved; boil gently till pumpkin is clear and syrup sets.

Raisin and Cranberry Jam *see under Cranberry.*

R

RASPBERRY CONSERVE (OR JAM)

910g (2lb) raspberries, 1.1kg (2½lb) sugar, water.

Clean and husk berries; put in pan with very small quantity of water to prevent sticking; bring slowly to the boil, stirring gently; add sugar, stirring till dissolved, boil for 3 min; pot and cover.

RASPBERRY JAM (Uncooked)

N.B. Use only perfect, dry and fresh-picked fruit.

450g (1lb) raspberries, 450g (1lb) sugar.

Warm sugar; mash raspberries and add to warmed sugar; stir continuously until sugar has dissolved; pot and cover. This jam thickens with keeping.

RASPBERRY JELLY

Raspberries, sugar.

Put raspberries in pan, crush with wooden spoon, heating very slowly; cook till soft; strain through jelly bag; put juice in pan with 800g sugar per litre liquid (1lb per pint), stirring till dissolved; bring to boil, cook fast 10–15 min to set; pot and cover immediately.

Raspberry Vinegar *see under Vinegars.*
Raspberry and Blackcurrant Jam; Raspberry and Blackcurrant
    Jelly *follow instructions for Raspberry and Redcurrant below.*
Raspberry and Gooseberry Jam *see under Gooseberry.*
Raspberry and Loganberry Jam *see under Loganberry.*
Raspberry and Peach Jam *see under Peach.*

RASPBERRY AND REDCURRANT JAM

910g (2lb) raspberries, 910g (2lb) redcurrants,
1.8kg (4lb) sugar.

Husk raspberries, stalk redcurrants; put both in pan and heat very slowly till juice starts to run; simmer 20 min; add sugar, stirring till dissolved; bring to fast boil for about 5 min or to set.

RASPBERRY AND REDCURRANT JELLY

910g (2lb) raspberries, 450g (1lb) redcurrants, sugar, water.

Put fruit in pan with water just to cover; simmer till completely soft; strain through jelly bag; put juice in pan with 800g sugar per litre liquid (1lb per pint), stirring till dissolved; boil fast to set; pot and cover at once.

RASPBERRY AND RHUBARB JAM

450g (1lb) raspberries, 450g (1lb) rhubarb,
910g (2lb) sugar, water.

Wash fruit, husk raspberries, trim and cut rhubarb; put in pan with minimum water; simmer very slowly till tender; add sugar, stirring till dissolved; boil fast to set. (If raspberries are fairly ripe, simmer rhubarb for about 10 min first then add the raspberries.)

Raspberries *see also Fruit Cockaigne, Mixed Fruit Jam, Tutti Frutti Jam.*

RED CABBAGE PICKLED

Red cabbage, salt, vinegar, whole peppercorns, allspice.

Remove outer leaves of cabbage and centre stalk and shred very finely; spread on plate, cover with salt, stand overnight; drain well, pack into jars; boil vinegar, peppercorns and allspice (2tsp. each to a litre vinegar/1tsp. per pint); cool slightly, pour over red cabbage to cover completely and seal down.

REDCURRANT JELLY

Redcurrants, sugar, water.

Put fruit in pan with water just to cover; simmer till completely soft; strain through jelly bag; put juice in pan with 600g sugar per litre liquid (¾lb per pint), stirring till dissolved; boil fast to set; pot and cover at once.

Redcurrant Vinegar *see Vinegars.*

Redcurrant and Blackcurrant Jam; Redcurrant and Blackcurrant
Jelly *see under Blackcurrant.*

Redcurrant and Cherry Jam *see under Cherry.*

Redcurrant and Gooseberry Jam; Redcurrant and Gooseberry
Jelly *see under Gooseberry.*

Redcurrant and Loganberry Jam; Redcurrant and Loganberry
Jelly *see under Loganberry.*

REDCURRANT AND MINT JELLY

Follow recipe for basic Redcurrant Jelly, adding good bunch of
fresh picked and washed mint during cooking before straining.

Redcurrant and Raspberry Jam; Redcurrant and Raspberry Jelly
see under Raspberry.

Redcurrant and Strawberry Jelly *see under Strawberry.*

Redcurrant *see also Fruit Cockaigne, Mixed Fruit Jam.*

RHUBARB CHUTNEY

Follow recipe for Apple Chutney (3) substituting rhubarb for
apples.

RHUBARB AND GINGER JAM (1)

*910g (2lb) rhubarb, 910g (2lb) sugar, 28g (1oz) root ginger
(bruised, in muslin bag).*

Wash and trim rhubarb and cut in small pieces; put in large bowl
with bag of ginger and cover with sugar; stand for 48 h; drain juice
into pan, bring to boil, stirring constantly and cook for about 15
min; add rhubarb, continue cooking till fruit is transparent, stirring from time to time; remove bag of ginger; pot and cover.

RHUBARB AND GINGER JAM (2)

450g (1lb) rhubarb, 450g (1lb) sugar, juice of 1 lemon,
1tsp. ground ginger, water.

Wash, trim and chop rhubarb; simmer in minimum water till tender; add lemon juice, ginger and sugar, stirring till dissolved; boil fast to set.

Rhubarb and Gooseberry Conserve *see under Gooseberry.*

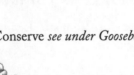

RHUBARB AND GRAPEFRUIT JAM

910g (2lb) rhubarb, 1 grapefruit, 910g (2lb) sugar.

Grate rind of grapefruit, core and pip and press fruit through coarse sieve; wash rhubarb, trim and cut in small pieces, put in bowl with layers of sugar, grated rind and juice of grapefruit; stand overnight; put in pan, bring to boil, stirring till sugar is dissolved; boil fast to set; pot and cover at once.

RHUBARB LEMON MARMALADE

1.4kg (3lb) rhubarb, 6 lemons, 1.4kg (3lb) sugar,
570ml (1 pint) water.

Squeeze juice of lemons, finely slice fruit, putting pith and pips in muslin bag; stand all in bowl with water overnight; put into pan with rhubarb, simmer for 20 min; add sugar, stirring till dissolved, bring to boil and cook steadily to set.

Rhubarb and Loganberry Jam *see under Loganberry.*
Rhubarb and Raspberry Jam *see under Raspberry.*

RHUBARB AND ORANGE MARMALADE

Follow recipe for Rhubarb Lemon Marmalade substituting oranges for lemons.

Rhubarb and Strawberry Jelly *see under Strawberry.*
Rose Vinegar *see under Vinegars.*

ROSE-GERANIUM JELLY (1)

Use a good basic jelly (i.e. apple, gooseberry, etc.), adding a good bunch of rose-geranium leaves in the first cooking and leave them to strain through the jelly bag with the fruit. A fresh washed leaf may be added to each jar when potting.

ROSE-GERANIUM JELLY (2)

Good bunch of rose-geranium leaves, 1.1kg (2½lb) sugar,
1large lemon, 1.1l (2 pints) water, ½ bottle commercial
pectin, 1tsp. allspice.

Wash rose-geranium leaves, put in bowl with sugar, allspice and lemon juice; stand for 1 h; put in pan with water, bring to boil, strain through coarse muslin; put liquid in pan with pectin, bring to boil for 1 min, pot and cover. A few drops of cochineal may be added to give colour, and a fresh washed rose-geranium leaf put in each jar.

ROSE-GERANIUM AND ORANGE JELLY

Follow basic recipe for Orange Jelly, adding a good bunch of rose-geranium leaves to the cooking before straining.

ROSEHIP JAM

450g (1lb) rosehips, 285ml (½ pint) water, sugar.

Simmer rosehips in water till tender; liquidize and/or sieve; put in pan with 1kg sugar per kilogram pulp (1lb per lb)and simmer till thick.

ROSEHIP JELLY

450g (1lb) rosehips, 910g (2lb) apples, 570ml (1 pint) water, sugar, lemon juice.

Chop apples, put in pan with 285ml (½ pint) water, simmer till pulped; strain through jelly bag; put rosehips in pan with the other 285ml (½ pint) water, simmer till soft; strain through jelly bag; combine both juices, put in pan with the juice of 1 lemon and 800g sugar per litre liquid (1lb per pint), stirring till dissolved; boil fast to set; pot and cover immediately.

Rosehips *see also Hedgerow Jam.*

ROSE PETAL JAM (1)

113g (4oz) rose petals, 680g (1½lb) sugar, 1tbs. lemon juice, 150ml (¼ pint) rose water (obtainable from chemists), 150ml (¼ pint) water.

Put sugar, water, rose water and lemon juice in pan and leave, stirring occasionally, till sugar is completely dissolved (without heating); add rose petals, stirring *continuously* over *very* low heat until petals are transparent; allow to cool slightly before potting.

ROSE PETAL JAM (2)

113g (4oz) rose petals, 680g (1½lb) sugar, 1tbs. lemon juice,
150ml (¼ pint) rose water, 150ml (¼ pint) water.

Put rose petals in bowl; put sugar, lemon juice, water and rose water in pan, bring to boil, simmer 5 min; pour over petals and stand overnight; put in pan, simmer very gently, stirring continuously for 30 min until syrup thickens.

ROWANBERRY JELLY

910g (2lb) rowanberries, 570ml (1 pint) water,
juice 1 small lemon, sugar.

Wash berries, simmer in water till tender; strain through jelly bag; put juice in pan with lemon juice and 800g sugar per litre liquid (1lb per pint); bring slowly to boil, then cook fast to set; pot and cover immediately.

RUM BUTTER

450g (1lb) butter, 450g (1lb) caster sugar,
150ml (¼ pint) rum, ½tsp. ground nutmeg.

Put sugar in bowl with nutmeg; add rum and stir till sugar is completely dissolved; melt butter in double saucepan, pour over rum and sugar, stirring till it starts to harden; pot and cover as for jam. (Well-stored, this will keep a long time, and so can be made well ahead for Christmas.)

S

SAGE JELLY

*56g (2oz) dried sage, 70ml (⅛ pint) vinegar, 680g (1½lb)
sugar, 1tbs. lemon juice, ½ bottle commercial pectin,
570ml (1 pint) water.*

Put sage in bowl, cover with 425ml (¾ pint) boiling water; stand
overnight; add 150ml (¼ pint) water, put in pan with vinegar,
sugar and lemon juice; bring to boil, stirring till sugar is dissolved;
boil fast for 5 min; remove from heat, add pectin, bring to boil for
1 min, skim if necessary; pot and cover at once.

Sage Vinegar *see Vinegars.*

SAMPHIRE PICKLE

*570ml (1 pint) samphire, 285ml (½ pint) cider, 28g (1oz) salt,
28g (1oz) grated horseradish, 14g (½oz) nasturtium seeds
and peppercorns.*

Wash samphire, drain well; put in jar with horseradish, peppercorns and nasturtium seeds; bring cider and vinegar to boil, add
salt, pour over samphire; put jar in warm oven for 1 h; cool and
cover.

SAUERKRAUT

N.B. A large container is needed for this with some form of lid
that can be pressed well down.

*White cabbage, kitchen salt, caraway seeds,
juniper berries or peppercorns.*

Wash cabbages, remove outer leaves and quarter; remove centre
core and hard stalks; shred very finely; line bottom of container
with clean whole cabbage leaves; then pack shredded cabbage
with a sprinkling of salt, caraway seeds, peppercorns or juniper berries, in reasonable layers until within 50mm (2in) of the
top; cover with clean cloth and lid, well weighted down; leave in
warmish place; when fermentation begins, scum daily, re-cover
with clean cloth, wash lid and weigh down again; when fermentation ceases, transfer to jars and seal down very closely.

Savory and Grape Jelly *see under Grapes (black)*.

SAVORY AND GRAPE JUICE JELLY

*1tbs. dried savory, 1 bottle dark grape juice, 680g (1½lb) sugar,
juice 1 lemon, ½ bottle commercial pectin.*

Put grape juice in pan with savory, heat gently till nearly boiling,
add pectin; bring to boil, add sugar and lemon juice; boil for 2
min, stirring constantly; remove from heat, skim as necessary;
pot and cover at once.

Shallots *see Onions.*

SLOE JELLY

Sloes, sugar, water.

Wash sloes and prick with needle; put in pan with water not
quite covering; bring to boil, simmer gently for about 2 h, strain
through jelly bag; return to pan with 800g sugar per litre juice
(1lb per pint), stirring till dissolved; boil fast for 10 min or to set;
pot and cover at once.

SLOE AND APPLE JELLY

450g (1lb) sloes, 450g (1lb) apples, water, sugar.

Wash and prick sloes with needle, cut up apples (do not peel or
core) and put both in pan with water not quite to cover; simmer
very gently till fruit is quite soft; strain through jelly bag; put liquid in pan with 800g sugar per litre juice (1lb per pint), stirring
till dissolved; boil fast to set; pot and cover when cold.

SHERRY SAUCE (VERY HOT)

285ml (½ pint) medium dry sherry, 56g (2oz) dried chillies.

Put together in screw-top jar and leave at least 1 month, shaking occasionally.

STRAWBERRY JAM

910g (2lb) strawberries, 680g (1½lb) sugar, juice 1 lemon.

Stalk fruit and remove any over-ripe berries; put in pan with lemon juice, heat very gently, stirring till boiling; add sugar gradually, stirring all the time, skimming as necessary; boil gently to set.

STRAWBERRY JAM (WHOLE FRUIT)

910g (2lb) strawberries, 680g (1½lb) sugar, juice 1 lemon.

Put sugar in pan with a little water to make a syrup; add lemon juice and strawberries very carefully; boil till syrup jellies; do stir *very* gently to avoid crushing the fruit.

STRAWBERRY JELLY

910g (2lb) strawberries, 285ml (½ pint) water, 1kg (2¼lb) sugar, 2tbs. lemon juice, ⅔ bottle pectin.

Hull strawberries, put in pan, crush well; add water and bring to boil; simmer 15 min with lid on; strain through thick muslin;

return juice to pan with lemon and sugar, stirring till dissolved; bring to fast boil for 2 min; remove from heat, stir in pectin, boil fast for 1 min; skim; pot and cover at once.

Strawberry and Gooseberry Jam *see under Gooseberry.*
Strawberry and Loganberry Jam *see under Loganberry.*

STRAWBERRY AND REDCURRANT JELLY

*450g (1lb) strawberries, 225g (½lb) redcurrants,
70ml (⅛ pint) water, sugar.*

Put fruit and water in pan; simmer till very soft; strain through jelly bag; return juice to pan with 800g sugar per litre liquid (1lb per pint), stirring till dissolved; boil fast to set; pot and cover at once.

STRAWBERRY AND RHUBARB JELLY

*450g (1lb) strawberries, 450g (1lb) rhubarb, 70ml (⅛ pint)
water, lemon, sugar.*

Hull strawberries, slice rhubarb; put in pan with water; simmer till very soft; strain through jelly bag; return juice to pan with juice of 2 lemons and 800g sugar per litre liquid (1 lemon and 1lb sugar per pint), stirring till dissolved; boil fast to set; pot and cover at once.

Strawberries *see also Fruit Cockaigne, Tutti Frutti Jam.*

Strawberries are a wonderful face wash; cut in half and rub over the face after normal washing or mix with tansy and milk and use as a lotion.

STRAWBERRY (WILD) JELLY

Wild strawberries, water, lemon, sugar.

Put berries in pan with juice of lemon and 500ml water for each kilogram fruit (1 pint per 2½lb); bring slowly to boil; simmer 10 min; strain through jelly bag; put juice in pan with 800g sugar per litre liquid, stirring till dissolved, boil fast to set; pot and cover at once.

T

TANGERINE CURD

6 tangerines, 1 lemon, 140g (5oz) butter, 280g (10oz) sugar, 3 medium eggs.

Put butter, sugar, grated rind and juice of tangerines and lemon in double saucepan and cook till melted and well blended; remove from heat; stir in well-beaten eggs, return to heat and keep stirring till thickened.

TANGERINE JELLY

910g (2lb) tangerines, 2 lemons, 1 grapefruit, 2.8l (5 pints) water, sugar.

Wash fruit, peel, and chop peel and fruit; put in pan with water and simmer till peel is soft (about 2 h); strain through jelly bag; put juice in pan with 800g sugar per litre liquid (1lb per pint), stirring till dissolved; boil rapidly for about 5 min or to set.

TANGERINE MARMALADE

10 tangerines, 1 lemon, 910g (2lb) sugar, water.

Halve tangerines, put pith and pips in muslin bag; put all in bowl, cover with 570ml (1 pint) boiling water; stand overnight; slice fruit thinly, add juice of lemon, make up liquid to 1.1l (2 pints); stand again overnight; put in pan, boil for 1 h; remove muslin bag; add sugar, stirring till dissolved, then boil gently for further hour or until set.

Tangerine and Grapefruit Jelly *see under Grapefruit*.
Tangerine and Lemon Marmalade *see under Lemon*.

TANGERINE AND LIME MARMALADE

9 tangerines, 3 limes, 1.4l (2½ pints) water,
680g (1½lb) sugar.

Wash fruit, squeeze juice, slice rinds as finely as possible; put fruit, juice and water in pan, bring to boil, simmer for 1 h or till rind is soft; add sugar, stirring till dissolved; boil for 5 min or to set.

THREE-FRUIT MARMALADE

3 Seville oranges, 3 large lemons, 2 large grapefruit, 2.7kg
(6lb) sugar, 3.4l (6 pints) water.

Wash fruit, squeeze juice, shred or mince rinds as desired; put pith and pips in muslin bag; put all in bowl with water and stand overnight; put in pan, simmer 2 h or till peel is soft; take out muslin bag, squeezing well, add sugar, stirring till dissolved, then boil rapidly for 5 min or to set. (There are many variations of this preserve – you can use sweet instead of Seville oranges or vary the quantities of individual fruits to your own particular taste.)

THREE-FRUIT AND GINGER MARMALADE

Follow recipe above adding 113g (4oz) bruised root ginger to the muslin bag, or 225g (8oz) sliced preserved ginger in with the fruit, or 2tsp. ground ginger per kilogram sugar (1tsp. per pound).

THYME JELLY

2tbs. chopped thyme, 70ml (⅛ pint) vinegar, 680g (1½lb) sugar, water, ½ bottle pectin.

Put thyme in bowl, cover with 285ml (½ pint) water and stand for 15 min; strain into pan, add vinegar and sugar; bring to boil, stirring till sugar is dissolved; remove from heat, add pectin, stir in well, boil for further 1 min; skim, pot and cover when cold.

THYME AND GRAPE JELLY

As for Savory and Grape substituting thyme for savory.

Thyme Vinegar *see Vinegars.*
Thyme *see also under Drying, page xxvii; Herbs, page 89.*

TOMATOES

As both green and ripe tomatoes have a number of recipes each, they are sub-divided into the two headings. Most greengrocers can supply green tomatoes at the end of the home-crop season, but contact them in good time to let them know you will be wanting them.

Green Tomatoes

GREEN TOMATO CHUTNEY

There are probably as many, if not more, recipes for this chutney than there are for apples, and the cooking principles can be the same.

Prepare tomatoes and other vegetables and fruit, chopped, minced or sliced as liked; put in pan with other ingredients (whole spices in muslin bag) and simmer gently till vegetables are soft and the mixture thickens.

(1) *910g (2lb) green tomatoes, 225g (½lb) cooking apples, 225g (½lb) stoned dates, 450g (1lb) soft brown sugar, 225g (½lb) onions, 570ml (1 pint) vinegar, 14g (½oz) garlic, 56g (2oz) salt, ½tsp. cloves, crushed allspice, crushed mustard seed, ground ginger, a few shredded chillies.*

(2) *910g (2lb) green tomatoes, 225g (8oz) onions, 225g (8oz) apples (peeled and cored), 225g (8oz) sugar, 285ml (½ pint) vinegar, ½tsp. salt, 1tsp. pickling spice.*

(3) *1.4kg (3lb) green tomatoes, 4 large cooking apples, 2 small cucumbers (sliced but not peeled), 3 large onions, 170g (6oz) sultanas, 340g (¾lb) dark brown sugar, 2tsp. dry mustard, 1½tsp. ground ginger, ½tsp. cayenne, 1½tbs. salt, 850ml (1½ pints) vinegar.*

(4) *1.1kg (2½lb) green tomatoes, 225g (½lb) onions, 225g (½lb) sugar, 1tsp. mixed spice, ½tsp. salt, 570ml (1 pint) vinegar.*

(5) *1.4kg (3lb) green tomatoes, 225g (½lb) cooking apples, 225g (½lb) onions, 113g (¼lb) prunes (soaked overnight and stoned), 170g (6oz) sugar, 425ml (¾ pint) vinegar, 28g (1oz) pickling spice.*

(6) *1.8kg (4lb) green tomatoes, 450g (1lb) sultanas, 225g (½lb) onions, rind and juice of 1 lemon, 910g (2lb) soft brown sugar, 850ml (1½ pints) malt vinegar, 1tbs. mustard seed, 2tsp. ground ginger.*

GREEN TOMATO JAM

450g (1lb) green tomatoes, 910g (2lb) sugar, 2tbs. lemon juice.

Wash and quarter tomatoes, put in bowl, cover with sugar; stand overnight; put in pan, simmer gently, stirring till sugar is dissolved and tomatoes are soft; add lemon juice and boil fast to set.

GREEN TOMATO JELLY

910g (2lb) green tomatoes, 570ml (1 pint) water, lemons, sugar.

Rough chop tomatoes, simmer in water to a pulp; strain through jelly bag; put liquid in pan with juice of 2 lemons and 800g sugar per litre (1 lemon, 1lb sugar per pint); stir till dissolved; boil fast to set. (This is a fairly sharp jelly and can be delicious with added herbs or spices.)

GREEN TOMATO MEXICAN RELISH

4 large green tomatoes, 2 green peppers, 1large onion, 2tbs.
chilli powder, ¼tsp. salt, 1tsp. grated horseradish, 570ml
(1 pint) white vinegar, 1tbs. dry mustard.

Put vinegar in pan, heat slightly, add chilli powder; simmer for
10 min; finely chop tomatoes, seed and finely chop peppers and
onion, mix all together with the horseradish and put in jar; add
salt and dry mustard to vinegar, bring to boil again and pour hot
over vegetables; cover tightly.

GREEN TOMATO PICKLE

Green tomatoes, salt, vinegar, brown sugar, cloves, peppercorns,
mustard seed.

Slice tomatoes and put in bowl with layers of salt; stand overnight; drain, put in pan with vinegar, sugar and spices (in muslin
bag) with 200g brown sugar, 12g each cloves, peppercorns and
mustard seed for each litre vinegar; simmer gently till tomatoes
are soft but not pulpy; cool, bottle and cover.

GREEN TOMATO AND APPLE CHUTNEY

Although several green tomato chutneys contain apple, the following two have a far higher proportion of apple to tomato.

(1) *225g (½lb) green tomatoes, 225g (½lb) sharp apples (when*
    peeled and cored), 225g (½lb) onions, 2 bananas, 225g (½lb)
    sultanas, 113g (4oz) crystallized ginger, 340g (¾lb) brown
    sugar, 1tbs. salt, 710ml (1¼ pints) vinegar.
(2) *1.4kg (3lb) green tomatoes, 1.8kg (4lb) sharp apples, 1.4kg*
    (3lb) onions, 450g (1lb) sultanas, 450g (1lb) preserved ginger,

6 pieces crushed root ginger, 2tsp. pickling spice, 680g (1½lb) dark brown sugar, 1tsp. salt, 1.1l (2 pints) vinegar.

GREEN TOMATO AND GINGER JAM

Follow recipe for Green Tomato Jam, adding 2tsp. ground ginger for each kilogram sugar (1tsp. per 1lb sugar). (This can be increased according to personal taste.)

SPANISH GREEN TOMATO CHUTNEY

680g (1½lb) green tomatoes, 225g (½lb) onions, 1 red pepper, 28g (1oz) salt, ½tsp. each peppercorns, mixed spice, mustard seed and cloves, 425ml. (¾ pint) vinegar, 170g (6oz) sugar.

Plunge tomatoes into boiling water, drain and skin them, then slice carefully; remove seeds from pepper and slice; finely chop onions, put in bowl, sprinkle with salt; stand overnight; drain; put in pan with vinegar and spices (in muslin bag), simmer for 10 min; add sugar, stirring till dissolved, simmer for 15 min, or till slightly thickened. This should be a crisp chutney.

GREEN TOMATO AND ORANGE CONSERVE

1.8kg (4lb) green tomatoes, 5 oranges, 2.3kg (5lb) sugar.

Put tomatoes and oranges through coarse mincer; put in pan with sugar, stirring till dissolved, then boil till thick and clear; pot and cover when cold.

Tomatoes (Green) *see also Indian Relish.*

Tomatoes

TOMATO CHOW-CHOW

6 large firm tomatoes, 1large onion, 1 green pepper, 56g (2oz) brown sugar, 28g (1oz) salt, 285ml (½ pint) vinegar.

Blanch, skin and finely slice tomatoes; rough chop onions; deseed and finely chop green pepper; put all ingredients in covered fireproof dish in slow oven till onion is tender; when cold, pot and cover closely.

TOMATO CHUTNEY

Follow the method of Green Tomato Chutney; for a pulpy texture, blanch and skin the tomatoes first.

(1) *910g (2lb) red tomatoes, 3 large onions, 3 green peppers, 570ml (1 pint) malt vinegar, 28g (1oz) salt, 113g (4oz) soft brown sugar, grated rind and juice of 1 lemon, ½tsp. each ground ginger, pepper and mace.*

(2) *1.8kg (4lb) red tomatoes, 225g (½lb) onions, 42g (1½oz) salt, 7g (¼oz) cloves, ½tsp. each cayenne and ground ginger, 84g (3oz) sugar, 285ml (½ pint) vinegar.*

(3) *450g (1lb) red tomatoes, 113g (4oz) onions, 113g (4oz) apple, 113g (4oz) sultanas, 113g (4oz) sugar, 150ml (¼ pint) vinegar, ½tsp. pickling spice, ½tsp. dry mustard, salt, pepper to taste.*

(4) *910g (2lb) red tomatoes, 910g (2lb) sugar, 225g (½lb) raisins, 570ml (1 pint) vinegar, 56g (2oz) salt, 21g (¾oz) garlic, 7g (¼oz) chilli powder.*

(5) *1.8kg (4lb) red tomatoes, 225g (½lb) sugar, 425ml (¾ pint) white vinegar, 28g (1oz) salt, 1tsp. cayenne, 28g (1oz) dry mustard, 3tsp. allspice.*

TOMATO HONEY

450g (1lb) red tomatoes, grated rind of 1 lemons,
sugar, lemon juice.

Rough chop tomatoes, put in pan with lemon rind; simmer till quite soft and nearly all liquid evaporated; liquidize, and/or sieve, put in pan with 800g sugar and juice 2 lemons per litre pulp (1lb sugar, juice 1 lemon per pint); stir till sugar is dissolved, boil rapidly till thick.

TOMATO JAM

910g (2lb) red tomatoes, 910g (2lb) sugar, 4tbs. lemon juice.

Quarter tomatoes, put in bowl, cover with sugar and stand overnight; put in pan, simmer gently, stirring till sugar dissolved; add lemon juice (juice 1 lemon, 1lb sugar per pint); boil fast to set.

TOMATO JELLY

910g (2lb) red tomatoes, sugar, 2 lemons,
285ml (½ pint) water.

Quarter tomatoes, simmer in water to pulp; strain through jelly bag; put juice in pan with juice of 2 lemons and 800g sugar per litre tomato juice, stirring till sugar dissolved; boil fast to set.

TOMATO MARMALADE

910g (2lb) red tomatoes, 2 lemons, 910g (2lb) sugar.

Plunge tomatoes in boiling water, drain and peel; slice; peel and slice lemons; put sugar in pan with a little water and stir over gentle heat till dissolved; boil to a syrup; add tomato and lemon slices, bring to slow boil, cook to setting point.

TOMATO PICKLE

1.4kg (3lb) red tomatoes, 450g (1lb) brown sugar, 570ml (1 pint) vinegar, 1 clove garlic, 1 blade mace, 1 stick cinnamon, tsp. allspice, salt.

Cut tomatoes in thick slices and stand in strong brine [150g salt to a litre water (3oz per pint)] overnight; drain carefully; boil vinegar and sugar; add tomatoes and spices, boil 2 min; remove tomato slices carefully, place in layers in jars; continue boiling vinegar till it thickens, then pour over tomatoes and cover closely.

TOMATO PRESERVE

450g (1lb) tomatoes, 450g (1lb) sugar, rind and juice 1 lemon, ground ginger or cinnamon to taste.

Blanch and skin tomatoes; put in bowl, cover with sugar; stand overnight; drain juice carefully into pan, boil to a heavy syrup; add tomatoes, rind and juice of lemon and spice, and cook till quite thick.

TOMATO RELISH – UNCOOKED

1.4kg (3lb) firm tomatoes, 3 large onions, 1 green pepper, 225g (½lb) celery, 225g (½lb) sugar, 570ml (1 pint) white vinegar, 56g (2oz) salt, 28g (1oz) mustard seed.

Peel, fine chop and drain tomatoes; fine chop onion, celery and green pepper; put all together in bowl with remaining ingredients, mix well, put in clean jars and seal. (Use the drained juice for flavouring a stew.)

TOMATO SAUCE

*680g (1½lb) ripe tomatoes, 113g (¼lb) onions, 285ml (½ pint)
vinegar, 56g (2oz) sugar, 2tsp. salt, 1tsp. dry mustard, pinch
cayenne, 4 cloves and blade of mace (both in muslin bag).*

Slice tomatoes, chop onions and put in pan with all other ingredients; simmer gently 1 h; put through liquidizer and/or sieve, return to pan, simmer to thickness required, stirring frequently; put in china bowl and when quite cold, put into screw-top bottles.

TOMATO AND APPLE CHUTNEY

*450g (1lb) each red tomatoes, apples and onions, 225g (½lb)
sultanas (or stoned raisins), 28g (1oz) pickling spice, 1tsp.
ground ginger, 425ml (¾ pint) vinegar, 225g (½lb) sugar.*

Finely chop onions, put in pan with half the vinegar and simmer till almost soft; blanch, skin and chop tomatoes; peel, core and chop apples; add both to pan with sultanas, salt, ginger and spices in muslin bag, and a little more vinegar if necessary; simmer till soft, stirring occasionally; add remaining vinegar and sugar, stirring till dissolved, then cook very slowly till thick; remove spice bag before potting.

TOMATO AND APPLE JAM

*450g (1lb) firm tomatoes, 340g (¾lb) apple (when peeled and
cored), 1 lemon, 680g (1½lb) sugar, water.*

Finely slice lemon, removing pips; put in pan with minimum water and simmer till tender; dice apples and slice tomatoes; add to pan with sugar, stirring till dissolved; boil till mixture is thick and clear; cool slightly before potting and cover when cold.

TOMATO AND HORSERADISH RELISH

*450g (1lb) firm red tomatoes, 2 large cooking apples, 1 large
onion, 2–3 tbs. grated horseradish, 450g (1lb) sugar, 425ml
(¾ pint) vinegar, 1tsp. salt, ½tsp. cayenne,
14g (½oz) pickling spice.*

Peel, core and rough chop apples, skin and chop tomatoes and
onion; cook *very* gently together to a thick pulp, stirring to prevent burning; boil together vinegar and pickling spice (in muslin
bag); add to tomato mixture with salt and pepper; simmer gently
till thick, add sugar, stirring till dissolved, and horseradish to personal taste; boil steadily for 15 min; pot and seal hot.

TOMATO AND MARROW CHUTNEY

*1.8kg (4lb) ripe tomatoes, 450g (1lb) marrow (when
prepared), 450g (1lb) onions, 340g (¾lb) sugar,
285ml (½ pint) vinegar, 1tsp. mixed spice,
14g (½oz) salt, pinch cayenne.*

Blanch, peel and quarter tomatoes; cut peeled and seeded marrow into cubes; rough chop onions; put all together in pan with
half the vinegar, salt, mixed spice and cayenne and cook gently till
tender; add remaining vinegar and sugar, stirring till dissolved,
then simmer till thick.

TURNIP CHUTNEY

*910g (2lb) turnips, 450g (1lb) apples, 450g (1lb) onions, 225g
(½lb) sultanas, 225g (½lb) moist sugar, 14g (½oz) turmeric,
1tsp. mustard, ¼tsp. pepper, 56g (2oz) salt,
1.1l (2 pints) vinegar.*

Peel turnips, cut in cubes and boil till soft; drain well and beat to pulp with wooden spoon; peel, core and finely chop apples and onions; mix turmeric and mustard with a little vinegar; put all ingredients in pan together and boil slowly for 1 h, stirring from time to time.

TUTTI FRUTTI JAM

*225g (½lb) each strawberries, raspberries, blackcurrants
and redcurrants, 910g (2lb) sugar, water.*

Prepare fruit; put blackcurrants in pan with very little water and simmer till tender; add other fruits; cook for about 10 min; add sugar, stirring till dissolved, boil fast to set.

V

Verbena and Lemon Jelly *see under Lemon*.

VINEGARS

When vinegar is stated in a recipe, malt vinegar is indicated unless otherwise stated, although at any time you want a lighter coloured pickle, relish or chutney use white vinegar. It is a little more expensive and not usually available in bulk quantities.

However, from time to time, you may come across various types of vinegar mentioned in the recipes, and sometimes it is pleasant to have flavoured vinegars for use with hors d'oeuvres and salads.

Spiced vinegar is listed first here, because it is so constantly used in pickling and chutney making that it is useful to have a bottle on hand ready for immediate use.

SPICED VINEGAR

570ml (1 pint) vinegar, 28g (1oz) pickling spice.

Boil together for 15 min; cool, strain and use as required.

FRUIT VINEGARS

450g (1lb) soft fruit, 570ml (1 pint) white vinegar, sugar.

Cover fruit with vinegar; stand 4–5 days, stirring occasionally; strain; put liquid in pan with 400g sugar per litre liquid (½lb per pint); boil for 10 min; bottle and seal. (Blackcurrants, redcurrants, raspberries, etc.)

HERB VINEGARS

Selected herbs, white or malt vinegar as required.

Crush herbs with rolling pin, half fill a jar and cover with cold vinegar; store for 6 weeks before use, shaking as often as possible, but at least once a week; strain before use. (Basil, marjoram, mint, sage, tarragon, thyme, etc.)

CHILLI VINEGAR

28g (1oz) chillies, 570ml (1 pint) vinegar, wine or malt.

Put together in bottle, shake frequently; after 3 weeks, strain and bottle.

CUCUMBER VINEGAR

1large cucumber, 1 onion, 1 shallot, 7g (¼oz) salt, 2tsp pepper, pinch of cayenne, 570ml (1 pint) white vinegar.

Peel and slice cucumber, slice onion and shallot; put in jar with remaining ingredients; stand for 1 week; transfer to pan, bring to boil for 3 min; allow to get cold, strain and bottle. (Don't waste the strained cucumber; make into a sauce to go with fish!)

GARLIC VINEGAR

56g (2oz) garlic, 570ml (1 pint) vinegar.

Boil vinegar and allow to get cold; finely chop garlic, add to vinegar and leave for 2 weeks; strain and bottle.

HORSERADISH VINEGAR

Horseradish, vinegar.

Wash, scrape and grate horseradish and half fill a jar; cover with cold vinegar; leave for six weeks, shaking often; strain before use.

LAVENDER VINEGAR

Lavender heads, white vinegar.

Steep lavender heads in white vinegar for 2 weeks on a sunny windowsill; strain before use.

ROSE VINEGAR

Fill glass jar with scented rose petals, cover with white vinegar, stand on sunny shelf for two weeks; strain before use.

The softly flavoured vinegars such as cucumber, lavender and rose are very pleasant for use with salad dressings.

W

WALNUTS PICKLED

Young walnuts, salt, vinegar and 1tbs. cloves, 1tbs. whole pep-
percorns and 2 onions for each litre (2 pints) vinegar.

Prick shells of young soft walnuts all over with steel needle; cover
with strong brine [100–140g per litre water (2–3oz per pint)];
stand for 10 days changing brine every two days; drain well
and dry in open air till black; boil vinegar with spices and finely
chopped onion; pack walnuts into jars; pour over strained vinegar
and, when quite cold, cover closely.

WALNUTS PICKLED SWEET

Follow recipe for Pickled Walnuts, adding 3½tsp. sugar per litre
spiced vinegar (1 tsp. per pint).

WATERMELON PRESERVE

*450g (1lb) watermelon rind, 28g (1oz) salt, 2.3l (4 pints)
water, 450g (1lb) sugar, 1 small lemon,
2tbs. sliced preserved ginger.*

Pare rind, removing all pink edge (use the fruit for breakfast); cut rind into cubes, put in bowl, cover with salt and 1.1l (2 pints) water; stand overnight; drain, rinse with cold water, drain again; put in pan, just cover with boiling water and cook for 15 min; add sugar and further 1.1l (2 pints) water; boil 5 min; add thin sliced lemon and sliced ginger; boil again for 2–3 min; pot and seal. (Unripe cantaloup or similar melons can also be treated in the same way.)

WATERMELON RIND PICKLED

*910g (2lb) watermelon rind, 113g (4oz) salt, 570ml (1 pint)
vinegar, 2.8l (5 pints) water, 1 lemon, 910g (2lb) sugar, 1tsp.
whole allspice, 1 stick cinnamon, 1tsp. cloves.*

Pare watermelon rind, removing any pink portion; cut into small pieces; put in bowl with salt and 2.3l (4 pints) water; stand overnight; drain, rinse with cold water, drain well; put in pan with 285ml (½ pint) water, boil till tender, add remaining ingredients (spices in muslin bag), stirring till sugar is dissolved, then boil fast till rind is clear; remove rind to jars; boil syrup further 5 min, pour on to rinds, then seal.

WHISKY SAUCE

½ bottle whisky, 113g (4oz) red chillies.

Put together in bottle, shake well once a week; do not use for 1 month. Use sparingly instead of tabasco sauce.

White Cabbage *see Sauerkraut.*

WHORTLEBERRY JAM

Follow recipe for Bilberry Jam.

WHORTLEBERRY JELLY

Whortleberries, sugar.

Wipe berries, put in fireproof dish with lid on, in slow oven till soft; mash with wooden spoon; strain through jelly bag; put juice in pan, bring to boil, add 800g sugar per litre juice (1lb per pint), stir till dissolved; boil 5 min or to set; pot and cover immediately.

WINE JELLY

150ml (¼ pint) dry sherry, 113g (4oz) redcurrant jelly, 150ml (¼ pint) claret, 2tbs. brandy, 28g (1oz) unflavoured gelatine.

Soften gelatine in sherry, dissolve redcurrant jelly, add sherry and gelatine, cool slightly, add claret and brandy; pot and cover when cold.

And to end the book –

XYZ – END OF SEASON RELISH

910g (2lb) green tomatoes, 2 medium onions, ½ small white cabbage, 2 red peppers, 2 green peppers, 225g (½lb) ripe tomatoes, 2 stalks celery, ½ cucumber, 850ml (1½ pints) white vinegar, 84g (3oz) salt, 1tsp. cayenne, 56g (2oz) dry mustard, 140g (5oz) sugar.

Prepare and chop all vegetables; put in a bowl, sprinkling salt between layers; stand overnight; drain well, squeezing out all liquid; put in pan with all other ingredients; cook gently for 1½ h, stirring frequently; pot and seal. (If you prefer a darker pickle use malt vinegar and brown sugar.)

This may be the end of a book, but it is by no means the end of a subject. There is so much still to be covered – syrups, ketchups (most of which need sterilizing before storing), sauces, even soups can be successfully stored. And as said before, bottling, canning and freezing are not even mentioned.

As the card index builds up from week to week, the whole subject becomes even more fascinating and covers such strange things as making shoe polish, dyes and disinfectants!

Quite apart from remembering the millions of people today who are on the starvation line and beyond, which makes it criminal to waste food of any description, the high cost of living can be greatly assisted by using everything we have around us, some of it for absolute free and a little bit of energy.

And don't forget, do experiment with mixing fruits and vegetables and flavours – the most astounding things can result quite accidentally. Mind you, there can also be some horrors too, but a little practice and even more ingenuity can make you the envy of many an accomplished hostess and 'your recipe' will be much sought after.